The Heart of Lord Ram

The Heart of Lord Ram

Reflected in Yoga Vasishtha

Daaji

Kamlesh Patel

JUGGERNAUT BOOKS
C-I-128, First Floor, Sangam Vihar, Near Holi Chowk,
New Delhi 110080, India

First published by Juggernaut Books 2025

10 9 8 7 6 5 4 3 2 1

P-ISBN: 9789353458935
E-ISBN: 9789353454289

The views and opinions expressed in this book are the author's own. The facts contained herein were reported to be true as on the date of publication by the author to the publishers of the book, and the publishers are not in any way liable for their accuracy or veracity.

Typeset in Adobe Caslon Pro by R. Ajith Kumar, Noida

Printed at Thomson Press India Ltd

Contents

Introduction xi
Reading the Yoga Vasishtha with Our Heart

Prologue xxi
The Yoga Vasishtha Chronicles Begin

The Four Gates of Liberation xxix

Gate 1: Contentment

1. Letting Go Makes Room For More 3
2. The Soul Does Not Lose 6
3. Peace Begins When Striving Ends 10
4. Stillness Is the Foundation of Change 14
5. Wholeness Comes When Longing Ends 19
6. Turiya Is the Rest Beyond Everything 26
7. Let Go of Even the Universe 30
8. Greatness Without Attachment 34
9. Real Peace Doesn't Depend on Place 39
10. Detachment Is Not Disconnection 44
11. Create Because It's Your Nature 50

Gate 2: Peaceful Self-Control

12. Carried Away by a Single Desire 59
13. What You Build Is Not Who You Are 65
14. The Effort to Let Go Is the First Freedom 69
15. Doubt Can Undo Everything 74
16. Desire Rehearsed Is Destiny Chosen 77
17. The Poise That Outlasted the World 82
18. Renunciation Is Inside the Action 87
19. Your Inner Impressions Shape the Next Life 90
20. From Pure Light to Form, and the Way Back 94

Gate 3: Discrimination Through Inquiry

21. The Mind That Dreamt a Lifetime 101
22. You Are Not the Role You Wake Up In 108
23. The Source Is Already Within You 115
24. You Have to Want the Truth, Not Just the Tools 119
25. Lives Come and Go, the Witness Stays 123
26. Wisdom Means Not Falling Again 128
27. When Identity Becomes the Obstacle 132
28. The Ego Is the Last Illusion 137

29. The Soul Is Buried Under What Is Imagined 141
30. What You Call God Is Still a Reflection 145
31. The World Becomes What You Believe 149
32. The Soul was Never Bound by the World 154
33. Stop Running, You're Already Home 161
34. Becoming One with the Spiritual State 167

Gate 4: Company of the Wise

35. Truth Doesn't Need an Audience 175
36. Stillness Within Action 182
37. Put the Heart Before the Mind 186
38. The Riddles That Silenced a Ghost 191
39. Worship Begins Where Form Ends 194
40. Freedom Needs No Beginning 198
41. Lead from the Soul, Not the Throne 204

Beyond the Gates – Arrival

42. The Seer Is Not What It Sees 211
43. Only the Self Remains 214
44. Remembering What the Soul Always Knew 218

Conclusion 223
After the Last Question

Appendices 230

वज्रादपि कठोराणि मृदूनि कुसुमादपि ।
लोकोत्तराणां चेतांसि को हि विज्ञातुमर्हति ।।

Illustrious and noble persons become firm like the 'Vajra' the weapon of God Indra and very gentle like a flower depending upon the prevailing situation. They are famous because of this special trait in them.

Introduction

Reading the Yoga Vasishtha with Our Heart

What is the point of it all?

That aching question asked by many young hearts today was also asked thousands of years ago by a teenage prince: Lord Ram, heir to the throne of Ayodhya. He had royalty, power and privilege. Still, he found himself restless and withdrawn. He began to wonder: Why do we suffer? Where does fear come from? Is peace possible in this world?

That moment of honest confusion became the beginning of one of the greatest spiritual conversations ever recorded. It was a dialogue about the nature of the mind, life and freedom between the young prince, Lord Ram, and his teacher, Sage Vasishtha.

This conversation became the Yoga Vasishtha.

The Yoga Vasishtha is a classical text from ancient India. It explores spiritual questions about life through stories, reflection and practical insight. It is a long and layered conversation between a restless teenager and a teacher who responds with clarity and perspective.

Two Princes, Two Paths

We all know how Prince Siddhartha once left his palace and spent years in solitude before becoming the Buddha. However, Lord Ram's path was different. He had a teacher in real time who could help him meet his inner crisis with wisdom.

Vasishtha had already lived through pain and loss. He had seen his ashram destroyed, lost his children and faced many trials. Through all of this, he had come to a clear understanding of life. Ram's questions became the channel through which that wisdom was shared.

A Twenty-Two-Day Transmission

What followed over the next twenty-two days was more than a lecture or discussion. It was a direct transmission of feelings and wisdom through stories, energy and understanding. In ancient traditions, 'transmission' means a sharing that flows from one heart to another through energy, presence, insight and attention, which could trigger feelings and wisdom in the recipient's heart.

This sharing took place in the royal court. Sages, family members and even celestial beings were present. Vasishtha used a unique approach. His stories were layered, with one tale inside another. Dreams turned into lifetimes, and time was not linear – it flowed in loops. What appeared as a fable held a key to inner clarity. Beneath every scene was the same inquiry: Who am I really? What is reality anyway?

Consciousness: A Field to Enter

The sages of that time did not use external tools like artificial intelligence (AI), visual graphics or videos. They relied on silence, observation and inner stillness. They paid attention to the way the mind works and how it affects the world inside and around us, how we can interiorize ourselves into the heart–mind field.

The Yoga Vasishtha is a guide to that inner world. These teachings have been brought forward for anyone standing at a turning point or asking, 'What now?'

Why This Book Now?

Ram was about sixteen years old when this conversation began. He had just returned from a journey with his brothers. They had visited sages, seen sacred forests and felt something new open within them. When they returned to the palace, the world they once enjoyed no longer felt real. The celebrations, the routine, the comfort – none of it made any sense or brought peace.

This kind of inner discomfort is familiar to many young people today. The outer world may appear fine. Life may seem busy and full. Still, the mind can feel tired and bored. There is pressure to perform, to fit in, to always appear okay. Many experience a feeling of restlessness or sadness that is hard to name.

Ram's questions came from that same space. Who am I? What is the meaning of life? Why do I feel this way even when nothing is wrong outside?

This book speaks to those questions with honesty.

Structure of the Book

There are many translations of the original Yoga Vasishtha, but this version speaks in the language of today. Just as it was first shared with a young Ram in his late teens, it is offered here for the same age group – older teenagers facing the challenges of modern life, with the same timeless wisdom, now in a voice they can relate to.

Here's how the book is built:

- The voice of Prince Ram tells the story with emotional clarity.
- Each story has Consciousness Keys that are epiphanies holding the essence.
- Each story ends with a section called 'Try This in Real Life', which begins with a modern

challenge or emotional situation that today's reader might relate to, such as stress, grief, comparison, uncertainty, social media burnout, overwhelm, etc. Then comes a simple, grounded practice: This may be a Heartfulness technique, a nature-based grounding method, a reflection tool or a journalling practice. The practice is followed by a short explanation of why it helps. This structure encourages awareness, emotional clarity and conscious inner action, which leads to understanding and eventually transformation.

Why These Gates? Why Now?

We live in a time of non-stop input. Messages, news, conversations, expectations – everything happens fast. Many feel emotionally overstretched. Some feel lonely even while being constantly 'connected'. Others are trying to hold everything together without knowing what they truly want.

The Yoga Vasishtha offers a space to step back and reflect, to understand what is happening inside. To guide Ram through his inner confusion, Sage Vasishtha taught four qualities, portals or stages called the Four Gates of Liberation:

1. Contentment brings steadiness in a world full of comparison.
2. Peaceful self-control helps us pause and act with balance.
3. Discrimination through inquiry helps us ask the questions that matter.
4. Company of the wise shows how guidance and friendship shape who we become.

Each story in this book explores one of these gates. Every practice is an invitation to try what Ram was learning. Some stories may feel unusual or surreal. They are written to stir something poignant. Through all of it, you'll stay close to young Ram, a boy who asks the same kind of questions many people ask today. His journey might help you understand your own.

How to Use This Book

You can read this book in many ways. You can read it in one go, cover to cover; or you can read one story a day or a random page. You can create a study circle. You may eventually decide to read it again and again.

The Consciousness Keys in each story are like lanterns holding the core insight in a single line. After the story, Try This in Real Life offers you a direct way to apply the insight. It begins with a modern predicament, then a practical step you can take and closes with why it matters. Some practices are experiential, like relaxation, cleaning and sky gazing. Others are reflective, like gratitude journalling and emotional inquiry.

You don't have to finish everything or master anything. What matters is the sincerity with which you reflect and try.

In ancient India, these teachings were shared in *satsang*s, gatherings where people listened together and learnt with open minds. This book continues in that spirit, offering a companionship and a togetherness.

From Insight to Action: A Note on 'Try This in Real Life'

Many, not all, of the practices in this book come from the Heartfulness lifestyle, including relaxation, meditation, cleaning, the Heartfulness prayer and specific detox tools like anger detox, stress detox and fear detox. These are simple and experiential.

Each one is introduced to help us navigate a relatable emotional or life situation. The goal is to turn insight into experience. Instructions for each are provided at the end of the book in the appendices.

If the Buddha had enjoyed a spiritual guide like Vasishtha, he may have created something like a Ram Rajya for the whole earth, a Buddha Bhumi perhaps. Maybe your generation or your grandchildren will still build it.

Read with your mind and you'll enjoy the stories. Read with your heart and you may meet yourself.

With love,
Daaji

28 November 2025

Prologue

The Yoga Vasishtha Chronicles Begin

I am Prince Ram.

You may already know parts of my story – the victories, the exile, the battles from the epic Ramayana. But before all of that, there was a moment that changed how I saw the world and my place in it. That is where this journey begins.

I was born in the great kingdom of Ayodhya as the eldest son of King Dasaratha. Initially, my father had no sons and longed for one. So, under the guidance of Sage Vasishtha, he performed the sacred Putrakameshti Yagna. From the divine fire, a celestial being appeared, offering a sacred nectar in a pot. My three mothers, Kaushalya, Kaikeyi and Sumitra, shared it and were blessed with four sons: me and my three brothers Lakshman, Bharat and Shatrughan.

We were inseparable at heart. We were brothers, warriors and companions. Life in Ayodhya was beautiful. We were surrounded with golden palaces, joyous celebrations and a world that seemed full of promise. If happiness could be bottled, Ayodhya had an overflowing supply. But even amidst all this splendour I felt restless.

As we grew older, we longed to see the world beyond the palace. To our surprise, our father agreed to let us travel. We visited great rishis, ashram-schools, sacred forests and rivers that seemed to whisper the secrets of time itself. We listened to sages who spoke of dharma, consciousness and the vastness of existence. It was awe-inspiring. We felt in harmony with nature, and a sudden uplifting of consciousness.

And then we returned home. That was when everything changed.

I should have felt joy at being back, but instead, I felt strangely empty. The laughter in the palace halls felt distant, the feasts excessive, the luxuries meaningless. My mind was restless.

I had felt and seen something on that journey. Something beyond the world I had always known. And now, I could not un-feel or un-see it.

What was the meaning of all this?

Then, fate intervened. Just when I was having my grand crisis, a great sage, Vishwamitra, arrived at our palace.

'My king,' Vishwamitra said to my father, 'I am performing a sacred ritual, but it is being disrupted by dark forces. I seek the aid of Prince Ram.'

My father hesitated. 'Ram is still young,' he said. 'He has never seen battle. And lately, he has been distant. I do not know if he is ready.'

'You see him as your son and a boy,' he said, 'but I see in my vision what he is destined to become – a great hero, a role model for all. This journey will awaken him.'

Sage Vasishtha spoke up, 'Your Majesty, this is no ordinary journey. Under Vishwamitra's guidance, Ram will gain knowledge of warfare and beyond. He will acquire wisdom and intuition that will shape his destiny.'

My father turned to me. 'Ram,' he said, 'will you do this?'

Before I could answer, Vishwamitra said, 'Your heart is troubled. What weighs on your mind?'

I hesitated, then finally spoke. 'What is the point of all this?' I asked. 'Life feels fleeting. We are born, we grow, we learn, and then one day, it all disappears. Everything we do, everything we build – all fades. What does any of it truly mean?'

It's the question that keeps philosophers awake at night and makes ordinary people stare at walls for hours. What does life mean? And, more importantly, will I ever get a straightforward answer?

Vishwamitra turned to Vasishtha and said, 'You are the person to enable him to find clarity and insight. Please go ahead.'

Vasishtha smiled, as if he had been waiting for this moment.

'Ah, Ram,' he said, 'you are standing at the door of something greater. The sorrow you feel is not an end. It is a beginning. The world you see is but a shadow of reality.'

And then, Sage Vasishtha began to speak of consciousness.

He said, 'You are not the waves, you are the ocean. Your emotions come and go. But your true self remains untouched, vast and infinite. Life is like a dream. While you're inside it, it feels real.

But when you wake up, you see it for what it truly is. What if waking up from this dream world is the real awakening?'

I listened, absorbing each word.

The world I had known – the palace, the festivals, the comforts – had always felt real. But what if reality was something else entirely?

Sage Vasishtha continued storytelling for twenty-one days.

On the last day, he said, 'Even consciousness itself is not the ultimate truth. It is merely a doorway. The great sages say, "Consciousness is all there is." But there are others who say, "Even consciousness is just a toy with which the enlightened play. Beyond it lies the source, the pure potential from which all things arise."'

That night, I could not sleep. My mind replayed Sage Vasishtha's words over and over. This journey was no longer just about protecting Sage Vishwamitra's rituals. It was the beginning of something far greater. And so, I left with Sage Vishwamitra, accompanied by my brother Lakshman. The sage gave me celestial weapons, each infused with divine power. But even more than that, he led me to a place that would change my life forever: the kingdom of Mithila.

It was there that I met Sita.

Before I could claim her hand, there was a test, a challenge that only the worthiest of the worthy could pass. A mighty bow, once wielded by the great god Shiva, rested in the court of Mithila's king, Janak. Many had tried to lift it, but none had succeeded. The bow was heavier than mountains, infused with divine energy. I meant to lift it, to string it. I didn't mean to break it, but it did. That moment sealed my destiny. Sita and I wed.

But life did not stop there. Exile. The forests. The trials. The war.

Sita was abducted by Ravana, the king of Lanka. I crossed an ocean, fought a battle, faced despair and discovered strengths I never knew I had. I led an army that belonged to another king, attained victory over Ravana and rescued my wife.

When we returned to Ayodhya, my reign was known as Ram Rajya where an era of righteousness and peace prevailed. I didn't know then that it would become the talk of the world for a long time. But none of it would have happened, if not for that one turning point in my life, the teachings of Guru Vasishtha: the Yoga Vasishtha, the knowledge of consciousness.

That was the understanding that life is more than what we see with our eyes. Over the course of twenty-two days, Guru Vasishtha shared stories of wisdom, of illusion and reality, of existence itself. They shaped me. And now, I want to share them with you.

These teachings will take you on a journey that will change how you see the world.

Yours,
Prince Ram

The Four Gates of Liberation

My teacher, Sage Vasishtha,* once told me how he came into being. In the early days of creation, the world was beautiful but chaotic. People had knowledge, but their hearts were confused. They performed rituals without purpose and understanding. Their minds were filled with longing. In response, Brahma entered into deep stillness,

---

*Before we begin the stories and teachings of the Yoga Vasishtha, it helps to understand who Sage Vasishtha was. He wasn't a scholar in the usual sense. He didn't grow into wisdom through study or experience. His clarity came from somewhere else, from something deeper, something already complete. So, who was he?

He was created by Brahma, the Creator, as a response to suffering.

The name 'Vasishtha' comes from the Sanskrit root vas, which means to abide, to dwell, to remain. The suffix -istha means the highest or most excellent. Thus, 'Vasishtha' means the one who has mastered dwelling in the Self. He lives in the truth that does not change and is established in consciousness, stillness and clarity. His name is a description of his heart's state.

and out of that silence, Vasishtha emerged to give direction to humanity.

On Mount Nishada, Brahma taught Sage Vasishtha that 'the one who teaches must be free from pride, desire, fear, anger and sin. Only such a being can quiet the storm in another's mind.'

During my time with Guru Vasishtha, he told me, 'There have been many Vyasas, Valmikis and Vasishthas, each born at different times, playing different roles and then returning to the ocean. Some liberated beings stay engaged with the world, but others withdraw.'

He explained that liberation cannot be achieved without effort. It is not given by birth or status. It comes through honest, consistent inner work. Even the great deities – Brahma, Vishnu, Shiva – reached their states through long practice and right action across many lives.

I asked, 'Then should I worry about my past?'

Vasishtha said, 'Right action in the present has the power to rise above the past. You are not bound by your story, but freed by your effort.'

I asked about failure. What happens when effort does not seem to bear fruit? Vasishtha said, 'That only means there is still some karmic debt. Keep going as good effort never goes to waste.' I asked, 'So is that fate?' He said, 'A lazy mind calls it fate. We call it fate when we don't want to take responsibility.'

Then I asked him about desire. 'What if I'm caught in it?' He answered, 'That's why you have intelligence, Ram. Use it. Know which desires bring peace and which do not. The mind is like a child. Guide it, but do not crush it. Even good desires will eventually fade away. Then what remains is peace.'

He told me that the knowledge he was passing to me had not begun with him. It was given to him by Brahma himself. When Vasishtha opened his eyes for the first time after being created, he asked Brahma, 'Why do beings suffer, and how can that suffering end?' Brahma gave him the path to liberation and instructed him to share it with those who were ready. For those who needed direction in daily life, he was told to teach the foundations, how to live, how to work, how to love and how to be decent. For those who had passed beyond material craving, he was to give the secret knowledge.

I asked, 'Why didn't Brahma send this wisdom from the beginning?' Vasishtha replied, 'Because in the early times, people were pure. Over time, their minds became corrupted, and rituals lost purpose and significance. That is when deeper knowledge had to descend, that consisted of the path of yoga, meditation, inner stillness.'

Then he told me something that has shaped everything that followed. At the gates of liberation stand four guards. The guards are:

- Contentment
- Peaceful self-control
- Discrimination through inquiry
- Company of the wise

All the stories that Vasishtha told me, as recorded in the text now known as the Yoga Vasishtha, can be understood through these four principles. Some stories reveal how inner control brings freedom and others sharpen inquiry, some create contentment and some show the power of noble company. These qualities interact with and support each other, and together they operate the field on which liberation can be strived for.

Contentment brings stability while inquiry sharpens the mind. Satsang, the company of the virtuous, makes the journey lighter. Peaceful self-control gives the space needed to act without compulsion.

Vasishtha gave me a metaphor. 'This body is a chariot. The senses are the horses. The breath is the wind. The mind of wisdom is the charioteer. And you, Ram, are the rider, the soul – silent, aware and eternal.'

He taught me, 'The pain of the world is healed only by meditation. Those who chase food and gold are like blind frogs in a dry well. But the one who has peace blooming in their heart, that person brings light to the world.'

He said, 'Be that lamp, Ram. Keep that peace. And aim for excellence.'

Vasishtha is more than just a sage, more than a wise, learned man. He is the one who abides in the Self, exactly as his name means. His teachings are the living continuation of the solution Brahma once gave.

In the stories that follow, we will meet kings, queens, sages, seekers and wanderers. But each one reveals the same truths: what binds us, and what sets us free. Their journeys follow the four gates of liberation. Each story will show how one of these qualities opens the way.

This is the path that was given to me. And now I will give it to you.

Yours,
Prince Ram

Gate 1

Contentment

1

Letting Go Makes Room For More

One day, I asked Vasishtha, 'Why do we suffer so much over things that are small? Why does a loss or a missed chance affect us more than it should?'

He said, 'Ram, even the smallest expectation can blind us. Let me tell you about a man who could not let go of a single coin, and almost missed a treasure.

'There once lived a merchant from the Kirata tribe. He was clever, calculating and very, very stingy. He rarely spent money as he believed every coin could multiply if invested carefully. Even though he had more than enough, his thoughts were always on getting more.

'One day, while walking through a forest, he dropped a single cowrie shell from his pouch. He panicked and searched for hours, and then for days. He combed the forest floor with the desperation of someone who'd lost a fortune.

'And then, by some strange grace, he found something else in the underbrush: a precious gem, far more valuable than the cowrie shell he'd been searching for.

'He stared at it in disbelief. He spent so much time chasing a tiny coin, but what he actually found was beyond anything he could have imagined.'

CONSCIOUSNESS KEY

Obsessing over what's gone can blind you to what's already arrived, if you're not conscious.

TRY THIS IN REAL LIFE

Relatable Situation

You studied hard for your board exams or university entrance test but didn't get the result you hoped for.

What To Do

Do Heartfulness relaxation as given in Appendix 1. Find a quiet place to sit or lie down. Go through your body, part by part, consciously releasing tension. Relax your toes, ankles, legs, spine, shoulders, neck and finally the face. Rest your awareness in your heart.

Why This Helps

Relaxation soothes the nervous system and clears the reactive emotional layer so you can begin again without panic.

2

The Soul Does Not Lose

Vasishtha once said, 'Ram, not all grief is sorrow. Sometimes, it's something greater, the heart growing bigger than it was before.'

Then he told me the story of Punya and Pavana, two brothers who shared the same loss. But their responses were different.

They were sons of Sage Dirgatapas, whose penance had illuminated him from the inside. He lived with his loving wife on the Mahendra mountain in a simple home filled with joy that comes from right living. Punya's name meant 'merit' and Pavana's name meant 'pure.'

Onc day, Dirgatapas, now over a 100 years old, left his body in meditation. His wife, whose heart was full of devotion, lay beside him and followed in his footsteps. Both passed away on the same day.

Punya, the elder son, sat quietly in grief. Pavana, the younger, wandered into the forest, lost in sorrow. Punya eventually found him, sitting by a river.

CONSCIOUSNESS KEY

Grief shows that something real once touched you. It's worth honouring.

Punya sat beside Pavana and said, 'I know your pain. But listen, our parents have gone to a place of peace. They have completed their journey. Your sorrow will not bring them back. Rather, it only stops you from continuing your journey.

'You have had thousands of parents from thousands of lifetimes. So have I. We've been swans, lions, camels, sharks, hunters and monks. Do you mourn the friends from those lives?

'This world is a stage and the roles keep changing, but the soul remains eternal.'

Pavana looked up. His eyes were tired.

Punya said, 'In this life, we are brothers. Let us honour this time together.'

CONSCIOUSNESS KEY

The soul does not die. It simply gets out of the body and moves on.

Pavana understood and he wept to let go of his grief. The two brothers walked home. In time, both of them were liberated after learning how to let go with love.

TRY THIS IN REAL LIFE

Relatable Situation

You recently lost a grandparent or a pet, or a close friendship that suddenly ended.

What To Do

Sit comfortably and gently close your eyes. Try the Heartfulness meditation as given in Appendix 2. Suppose that the source of divine light is present in your heart and it is drawing you inwards. Remain with that feeling. If your attention drifts, gently return to your heart. Meditate for fifteen to twenty minutes.

Why This Helps

Meditation helps you reconnect with your heart, to what is permanent inside you. You feel that you are not just the body but also the soul within.

3

Peace Begins When Striving Ends

After one of Vasishtha's teachings, I said to him, 'You speak of peace. But why is it that even after giving everything up, we may still feel restless?'

He said, 'Because giving up is easy. To quiet what is inside needs courage. Let me tell you about Vitahavya.'

Vitahavya was a scholar of rituals and was an expert in fire offerings, chants and sacred rituals. He was praised in temples and honoured in courts. But one day, he stopped as everything felt meaningless to him.

He gave up his rituals and went to a mountain cave in the Vindhyas with one aim, which was to find lasting peace. He meditated for long hours, trying to shut out the world and let go of everything he was attached to. But no matter what he did, his mind remained restless.

He said, 'I have restrained my outer organs. But my mind is still restless.'

CONSCIOUSNESS KEY

The mind is regulated when we stop giving attention to every thought.

So Vitahavya turned his attention to the heart. He understood that the mind and senses have no power of their own without the support of the soul. The ego may say, 'I am the doer,' but ego is only the tool; it is the mind that decides whether that tool is used for good or harm. He saw that it is wiser to let go of the desires that exhaust the mind rather than keep chasing them until the mind breaks down.

For 300 years, he remained in that cave, covered in mud and untouched by time. When his meditation was complete, he tried to get up, but his body was caked in mud and he could not lift it. So he whispered, 'This body is neither loss nor gain. Let the soul rise.'

And his spirit lifted towards the sun. Solar force poured down as rain in return, dissolving the dirt from his body. When he stood again, he washed himself in the river. Then, one by one, he bade farewell to every part of his identity: his roles, his memories, even his name. Finally, he attained liberation.

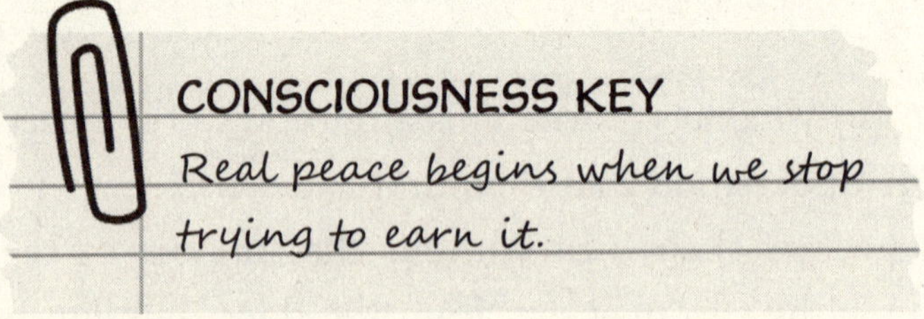

Hearing this tale, I asked Vasishtha, 'What must I give up to be free, in this life or the next?'

He answered, 'Slowly give up all desires, even the subtle ones, as to how life should feel. Don't chase pleasure or run away from pain. Don't be lifted by hope or crushed by disappointment. Do your duty with an open mind and a joyful heart. And let your intelligence serve your spirit, not your ego.'

TRY THIS IN REAL LIFE

Relatable Situation

You've been stuck in an endless cycle of trying to improve. You go to the gym, you journal, you try your best to inculcate good habits. But you still feel tired inside.

What To Do

Try the Heartfulness cleaning from Appendix 3. Close your eyes and gently suggest that all heaviness and anxiety are leaving your body through your back like smoke. After twenty minutes, feel a current of lightness or life from the source entering your heart from the front.

Why This Helps

Cleaning removes emotional clutter and resets your system, allowing peace to arise naturally.

4

Stillness Is the Foundation of Change

Vasishtha once said, 'Ram, not all grief leads to sorrow. Some grief becomes soil, and in it, wisdom grows.'

Then he told me the story of Dasura, the son of a sage, who climbed a tree to heal his heart and never came down.

Dasura's father, Sharaloma, was a noble sage. When he died, the forest wept silently, and so did Dasura.

He grieved for a long time. The woodland spirits, sensing his pure heart, came to console him. One spirit whispered to him what sages always know but hearts forget: 'Everything born must die. But from every passing, something sacred is born again.'

Dasura performed the final rites for his father's body, but his grief remained. He didn't want to meditate on the earth that had seen so much grief. So he prayed to the god of fire: 'Give me a space untouched by people's pain, a tree born from purity, so I can sit on its branch and find what cannot die.'

The fire god heard him. A great kadamba tree appeared. It was luminous, calm and strong. Dasura climbed onto its branches, chose one wide enough to hold him and began his meditation.

CONSCIOUSNESS KEY

Some silences heal, but others become a space where the soul begins to see itself clearly.

Many years passed. One day, as he emerged from meditation, he saw a forest goddess bowing before him. She said, 'All other spirits of the woods have children. I do not.'

He taught her to meditate and in time, she bore a son.

She raised the child and taught him worldly skills, like how to speak, build, trade and live among others. And when he turned twelve, she brought him back to the tree. Dasura taught him what his mother did not. Together, they meditated, lived and grew, all within the shelter of the tree. The tree gave them food, comfort and peace.

Dasura had now become a teacher in his own right. When Vasishtha arrived, he sat with Dasura under the tree and listened to a story. Dasura spoke of King Khottha, a king born of air who ruled a vast city filled with moving bodies. These bodies had five senses and nine gates, and a god of ego stood guard over them. Whenever desire built up, the king built a new body, a new palace and left the old one behind.

The boy, the child borne by the forest goddess in Dasura's presence asked, 'What does this mean?'

Dasura replied, 'The king is the mind. The city is this body. The god of ego stands watch. The mind, driven by desire, keeps building new bodies. When one life ends, the mind simply walks into another.'

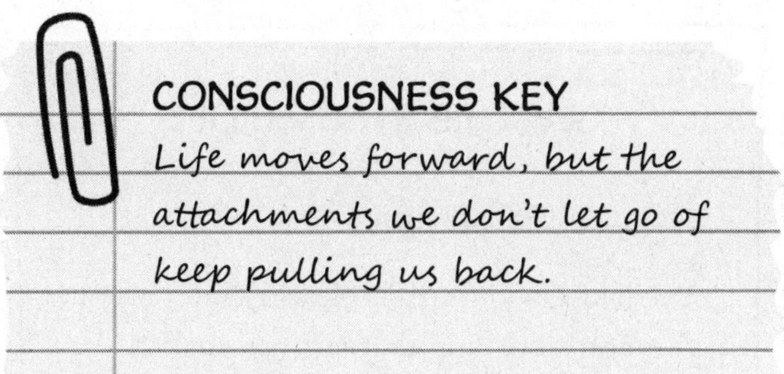

Dasura continued, 'Desires begin within, but if you stop feeding them, they lose strength. What you carry inside shapes how you see everything around you. So place your attention on the part of you that is simply watching.'

And the boy listened.

Vasishtha had come to visit, but he stayed to learn. And when he left, he bowed to not only Dasura but also to the tree that had given shelter to a boy, a goddess, a student and to silence that could teach.

TRY THIS IN REAL LIFE

Relatable Situation

You had a fallout with a close friend or went through a breakup that left you shaken.

What To Do

At bedtime, sit comfortably and silently offer the Heartfulness prayer as mentioned in Appendix 4. Let the words settle in your heart. Repeat the prayer once or twice as you slip into deep sleep.

Why This Helps

Prayer opens space for emotional release and trust. It calms the heart without needing to resolve everything.

5

Wholeness Comes When Longing Ends

In a distant part of the world, there lived a mighty king named Vipaschit. He was wise, noble and radiant, known for his unwavering devotion to Agni, the fire god, who was a friend and guide.

One day, a series of messengers, brought news about the commanders of his army from all four directions – East, West, North and South. The commander of the East had died of a sudden fever. The commander of the South had been killed in battle. The North was overrun and its leader had fled. And finally, the commander of the West arrived in person, wounded, weary and full of defeat.

King Vipaschit gathered his remaining generals and told them to prepare the last line of defence.

But first, he went alone to the temple of Agni to offer his final prayer.

'All my life,' he thought, 'I kept our enemies at bay. Now that I am old and frail, they rise again. I cannot fight as I once did. Let me offer this old body into your flames, O Agni. In return, give me four youthful bodies, born from my soul, so they may defend this kingdom.'

With calmness, Vipaschit entered the fire. As his body was consumed, four young princes leapt forth from the flames, who were strong, radiant and armed for battle.

The four princes rode out in different directions, each facing overwhelming enemy forces. But with faith, courage and unity of soul they invoked the mystical missiles of Paryaya, which turned the tides of battles, and Vayavya, the wind weapon that scattered the enemy like leaves. Together, these forces broke the siege on all four sides.

After their victory, the four soul-brothers went their separate ways. Each lived through danger, joy and strange fates, yet remained connected with the other three by an invisible thread of shared consciousness.

One became a tree, because he was cursed by a sage. Another, a stone, bound by ghostly pisachas, who are ghostly demons. One offered meat to appease the spirits and free his brother. Another was reborn as a bull, and later on as a lion. Again and again, one came to save the other.

Though they lived many lives, their souls were neither fully bound nor fully free. They had glimpses of wisdom, but also clung to passion, longing and memory. Eventually, each of them died in a different way. One was swallowed by a shark. The other was burnt by Indra. Yet another was crushed by an elephant. And one fell in battle with a Rakshasa.

Each soul went in a different direction after death. One prayed and received divine wisdom from Lord Vishnu. He meditated, transcended his attachments and attained nirvana.

But the others wandered. One still imagined himself to be a king, enjoying sensory pleasures in a dream-like body. Yet another was again swallowed by a shark, but this time killed it from within, journeyed to the mountain of gods and became a deva. And the final prince, still full of desires, meditated on the moon, saw the image of a deer and became a deer.

CONSCIOUSNESS KEY

Wisdom gets distorted when desire is still present. True freedom comes only when the very last longing has faded.

That deer was later presented to Vasishtha by a nobleman from Trigarta. When he saw the animal, he recognized the soul within it. He explained that one part of King Vipaschit's soul, after many lifetimes, had remained bound by lingering desires, taking the form of a deer.

Thus, Vasishtha shared the tale of the king who had become four, with each fragment of his soul living through different experiences across many births, until one part continued to wander in the body of this deer.

I felt compassionate and asked, 'How was he restored to his true form?'

Vasishtha replied, 'Only the path that once lifted him could lift him again. Vipaschit was a worshipper of fire. So, fire had to call him back.'

Vasishtha had meditated, chanted sacred mantras and sprinkled water. A great flame rose up and the deer leapt into it on its own. Vasishtha prayed to Agni, 'Remember the king who served you with devotion. Restore him now.'

From the heart of the flame stepped a radiant figure, clothed in white robes, shining with brilliance. The people called him Bhasa, meaning 'light'.

Bhasa bowed to Vasishtha and shared the memories of his many lives: tree, swan, jackal, bull, lion. All were awestruck.

Vasishtha blessed him, 'May your ignorance vanish forever.'

Bhasa, now fully restored, spoke of how life across different realms and worlds follows a pattern, much like the journey of Vipaschit's soul.

He said, 'Life spins in vast patterns. The earth, round like a sugar ball, is traversed by countless beings like ants, each believing their way is the ultimate one. A race called the Vatadanas, for instance, once set out to find the ends of the world. They walked from land to sea, from sky to sky, but never found an edge. They, like ants, still wander, thinking they are close to the truth.'

Bhasa continued, 'There are planets without scriptures where beings simply know right from wrong by feeling it within. Worlds without women, yet new life still emerges. Floating palaces that travel through space and land on ground. Realms where men, animals and even alien forms exist with a oneness, seeing everything as a part of the same divine essence.'

He then shared something profound: 'In our existences, there are planes without time or memory, only space and silence, where past, present and future melt into eternity.'

CONSCIOUSNESS KEY

All is connected, and life unfolds in cycles, tied by the thread of one shared consciousness.

TRY THIS IN REAL LIFE

Relatable Situation

There's someone you feel uneasy around. They may have misjudged you, hurt you or perhaps you've never understood each other. You keep trying to move on, but the tension or anxiety still lives inside one or both of you.

What To Do

Practise seeding positive thoughts mentioned in Appendix 10. Sit quietly and bring this person gently to mind. Think of them as your well-wisher. Each time you breathe out, imagine particles of peace flowing from your heart to theirs. Each time you breathe in, release any fear, defensiveness or judgement you may be holding and throw them out. Practice for a few minutes daily for at least a week.

Why This Helps

The memories that we carry have emotions tied to them. Even when a relationship changes or ends, the emotional trace can stay with us for years. This practice clears the layer of reaction left behind. Bhasa's many lifetimes left unresolved desires and impressions. His return to wholeness came only when those were released. This practice works the same way, it helps restore clarity where something unfinished still lingers.

6

Turiya Is the Rest Beyond Everything

One day, Guru Vasishtha looked at me and said, 'Ram, there are three bodies you carry through this life. One is your physical body, made from food. The second is your mental-intellectual body, shaped by thoughts, desires and memory. And third is your spiritual body, which is eternal and undisturbed. Learn to rest in that third one, which is your real support.'

'Gurudev, I shall surely do as you say. However, I have a question: I know the three states: waking, sleeping and dreaming. But what is this fourth state, Turiya, that you have hinted of in the past?'

He replied, 'Turiya is not a thing to understand. It is the absence of doing. It is where even existence and non-existence dissolve. There is no "I" and no "not-I", just pure witness-hood.'

And then, to help me feel it, he told me this story:

Once there was a hunter who had wounded a deer. He chased it into the forest and saw a sage sitting silently under a tree.

The hunter asked, 'Did a deer pass this way? It was hit by my arrow.'

The sage replied, 'I do not know. I was resting in the fourth state, the state beyond waking, sleeping and dreaming. In that state, I see nothing and react to nothing. I am sorry, I cannot help you.'

The hunter walked away, confused. But the sage was not confused. He was free.

Something about this story struck a chord in me.

Vasishtha looked at me and said, 'Be like that sage, Ram. Don't let the senses drag you into reaction. Live life with inward stillness, as if you "appear" sleepwalking through action, unattached. It may look like death to the outsiders, but actually life within is untouched by decay.'

CONSCIOUSNESS KEY

Real rest is found in the place where even the dreamer is absent.

TRY THIS IN REAL LIFE

Relatable Situation

You've been socially overloaded with too many events, chats and calls.

What To Do

As mentioned in Appendix 8, do left-nostril breathing. Block your right nostril and breathe slowly through the left nostril for five minutes. This activates the calming energy.

Why This Helps

Turiya isn't a state you reach by effort. It's revealed when outer and inner noise settle. Left-nostril breathing slows the nervous system and quiets the mind, creating the space needed to notice what remains when all mental activity drops. It doesn't take you to Turiya directly, but it helps remove what keeps you from resting there.

7

Let Go of Even the Universe

Once, I asked Vasishtha, 'Is it possible to hear something beyond thought? Something that leads us outside time itself?'

Vasishtha replied, 'Yes, Ram. Let me tell you of such a journey I once undertook.

'One day, I heard a sweet, mysterious sound. It wasn't music exactly; it was more like a voice calling from beyond the edge of thought. I followed the sound across forests, hills and skies. But I couldn't find where it was coming from. So I let my breath settle, entered a trance and stilled my body and mind completely. Then my spirit body lifted out of the known world and entered the space between worlds. I began to see things that had no beginning or end, worlds within worlds, and countless Rams, Vasishthas and sages like shadows repeating across time.

'I realized that all of it – space, time, form – is a play of the mind.'

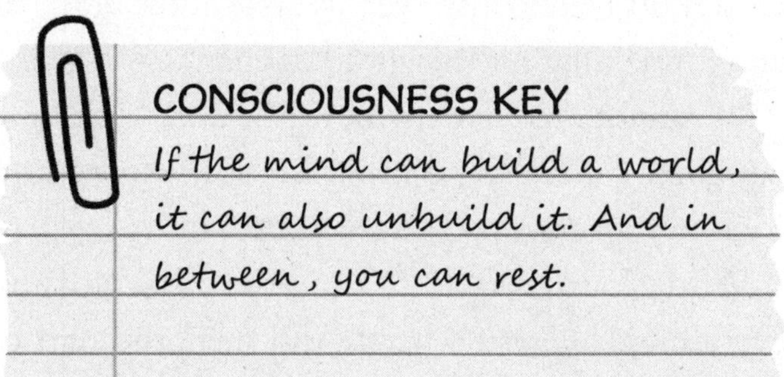

'As I journeyed through these realms, a luminous woman approached me. She sat near me and spoke gently. "I am a Vidyadhari," she said. "My husband created me by his mind-power through prayer, he longed for companionship and shaped me from his own longing. But once I came into being, he disappeared into his meditation and forgot me. I love him still, but I am stuck, half-longing, half-light."

She showed me how she lived, as an ethereal presence inside stone. She took me to her husband, still seated in meditation.

She said, "Please guide us both towards liberation. I want peace, not more longing."

I didn't know what to say. Then her husband opened his eyes. He told me that the Creator had already decided to dissolve this cycle of the universe, and it was time for the world to end.

"I cannot help her anymore," he said. "The time has come for me to go inwards. And you must go back to your own path, Vasishtha."

And then, I saw it: the final dissolution, everything collapsing back. And then, the start of a new creation, as if nothing had happened. Like an exhale before a new breath.

I returned to my sky-home in spirit form. There I found a Siddha, a radiant sage, just as he started to fall from the sky.

We laughed, sat together and shared what we had each seen. Then we soared through the sky, above all worlds, and dissolved into understanding.'

CONSCIOUSNESS KEY

When our attachment to 'how things should turn out' dissolves, peace evolves into poise, that is timeless.

TRY THIS IN REAL LIFE

Relatable Situation

You're addicted to planning everything – your career, next steps, your future five years from now – because you are fearful of how things would turn out to be if you do not have a plan.

What To Do

Use the guided Ocean of Peace from Appendix 6. Sit down, close your eyes and allow waves of peace to wash over your worries, fears and anxiety.

Why This Helps

This releases tension and shows the body what letting go feels like.

8

Greatness Without Attachment

I had always heard that King Bhagiratha brought the sacred Ganga to the earth to redeem his ancestors. But what Vasishtha told me revealed something greater, something rarely spoken about.

'Ram,' he said, 'Bhagiratha did not begin as a hero, but as a renunciate, like a Buddha. You may wonder – wasn't Buddha born much later? But know this: in every age, a Buddha arises, one who embodies that spirit of renunciation. Bhagiratha belonged to that stream. And yet, he went even beyond the Buddhas of his time. When fate pulled him back into kingship, he didn't resist but accepted it calmly. He ruled, but remained unattached and that is the mark of the highest success.'

We began at the beginning.

Bhagiratha was a king so noble that people could hardly believe he was human. He gave without hesitation and served with joy. He cared for the smallest detail and never once turned away someone in need.

But inwardly, he was tired. Despite all success, his heart felt barren. 'Every day feels like a loop,' he told his teacher Tritala. 'I cannot bear this emptiness. Is there a way to be free from this craving?'

Tritala replied gently, 'Yes. The way is through the joy of the soul. It comes with non-attachment. Through awareness of the truth, and the freedom from ego.'

Bhagiratha asked, 'But how?'

His teacher answered, 'Only when your mind realizes the truth through meditation, contemplation and surrender can it reflect the soul clearly. Only then does rebirth end and only then can fear vanish.'

Then Tritala asked the question that would change Bhagiratha forever, 'Can you give up your kingdom, your status, your wealth, even your fear of what others will say? Can you become like a beggar in front of your enemies and still walk with courage?'

Bhagiratha replied in action. He gave away everything, his palaces, gold, land, title. He walked away with the wisdom of his soul. Once, when he wandered into his old capital, the people wept and begged him to return. He took only one meal and walked on.

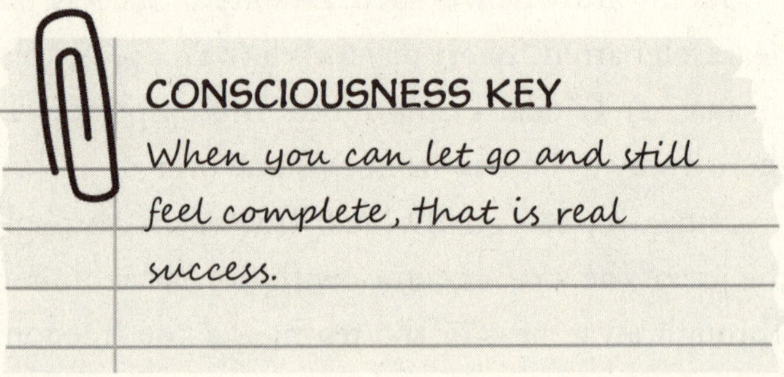

Then came the turning point in his life. A distant kingdom lost its ruler. The people of the land turned to Bhagiratha and begged him to become their king. He accepted it as a response to dharma. Later, his original kingdom also called him back. Now, he ruled over a vast land, but still felt no attachment, only a sense of duty.

Yet he had one sacred longing – to redeem his ancestors who had perished under a curse. He performed penance and brought Mother Ganga to the earth to bless their ashes. Bhagiratha lived a life of renunciation, strength, love and perfect detachment. His devotion to duty was his nobility.

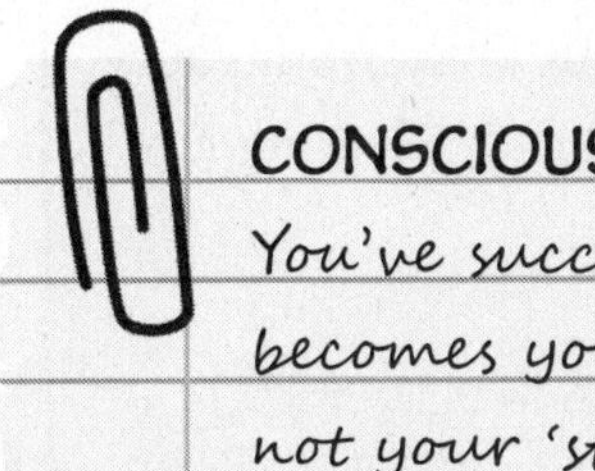

CONSCIOUSNESS KEY

You've succeeded when service becomes your 'innate nature', not your 'strategy'.

TRY THIS IN REAL LIFE

Relatable Situation

You were praised for something, like a project, a role or a performance, and now you're worried about messing it up next time. It feels like everyone's watching, and the pressure to keep being 'great' is making you tense inside.

What To Do

Do Heartfulness relaxation as given in Appendix 1 and let awareness travel through each part of your body, from your toes to the top of your head, releasing any tightness.

Why This Helps

Praise can feel good, but it creates pressure to repeat, perform or protect a reputation. That pressure turns into fear, like the fear of not meeting expectations. This practice helps release that internal tightness.

By relaxing the body and bringing attention inwards, you shift from needing approval to being present. Just like Bhagiratha served with excellence but stayed free from outcome, this helps you stay effective without carrying the weight of it.

9

Real Peace Doesn't Depend on Place

One day, I asked Vasishtha, 'Is there any person who truly lived in complete freedom, ruling a kingdom but untouched by power, able to accept both heaven and hell without flinching?'

He smiled. 'Yes, Ram. There was one. Let me tell you the story of Maha Bali, the asura king who was so much at peace that even losing the heavens did not worry him.'

Maha Bali ruled a vast empire in the lower realms, lands inhabited by Nagas, Yakshas and other powerful beings. His conquests were legendary and his wealth was unimaginable. No king or warrior could defeat him.

But one day, he no longer felt any joy. He remembered something his father Virochana had told him when he was young. He had asked, 'Father, is there a state where pain and pleasure no longer disturb the mind, and where peace is permanent?'

Virochana answered with a metaphor, 'Inside you is a land ruled by a minister who controls everything and not even gods can defeat him. He can be brought under control only when the true king appears.'

Confused, Bali asked, 'Who is the minister and who is the king?'

Virochana said, 'The mind is the minister; the soul is the king. The mind chases ego, comfort and distraction. But when you keep your attention on the soul through discipline and focus, the mind settles and peace follows.'

Bali sat down in silence and focused inwardly on his teacher, Shukracharya. In those days, messengers weren't needed. A clear thought and sincere longing was enough, like telepathy. Shukra heard this inner call from Bali and came to him.

Bali said to him, 'I feel no joy in conquest and my hunger for victory is gone.'

Shukra said, 'Everything you seek – joy, peace, power – comes from consciousness. That's the true treasure. But don't run away from your duties. Keep serving the world with full awareness.'

Then Shukra departed.

Bali turned fully inwards. He meditated so deeply that his entire being glowed. His ministers didn't know what to do. When they called Shukra back, he simply looked at Bali and smiled.

'Leave him be,' he said. 'He has crossed the storm and is free. Rule in his name until he returns.'

Years passed. One day, noise from the royal hall stirred Bali from his stillness and he opened his eyes.

He thought, 'I have no desire. No aversion. Whether I meditate or govern, it makes no difference. Let me serve without preference.'

And so he ruled again. But now, nothing disturbed him – not praise, not insult, not victory, not loss.

Even when Vishnu, disguised as a humble priest, came and asked for Bali's kingdom on behalf of Indra, Bali gave it away with a calm smile.

'Take it,' he said. 'It is not mine.'

Later, Vishnu offered him another kingdom.

Bali accepted, just as lightly. To him, heaven and hell were the same. His joy came from the state of being he carried within. Wherever he was, that place became heaven.

CONSCIOUSNESS KEY

Real success comes from being ruled by the heart.

TRY THIS IN REAL LIFE

Relatable Situation

You are in a new place or position. When people expect things from you, you get affected by things like approval, criticism, changes in plan, etc., even when you do your part.

What To Do

Sit down in a quiet place and close your eyes. Bring your attention to your heart, where you can sense a universal centre operating from within. If your attention drifts, return it to the heart. Continue for ten to fifteen minutes.

Why This Helps

In new situations, it's easy to get affected by approval, pressure or doubt. This practice trains your attention to rest in the heart, the place Virochana called the true seat of the soul. That's where clarity begins and where outer roles lose their control. Like Bali, you begin to act without craving results. Whether you lead, follow or let go, the sense of balance stays the same.

10

Detachment Is Not Disconnection

Once, Sage Vasishtha noticed my disturbed expression and asked, 'You seem troubled, my dear prince. What weighs on your mind today?'

I folded my hands, bowed respectfully and said, 'Gurudev, you have told me about renunciation, detachment and letting go. I have been thinking if it is possible to live in the world, love people, dream big and still be detached. Does peace mean walking away from everything? Do I have to let go of my family, my brothers, my duties?'

'Ram,' he said, 'do you think a bird is free because it abandons its nest? Or because it knows how to fly?'

I blinked. 'Well, it's the flying that makes it free, not the leaving.'

He nodded. 'Exactly! Real renunciation isn't about escape but about elevation. It is to rise above without cutting off and to be in the world but not get caught up by it.'

Then he said, 'Let me tell you a story about a king and a queen who asked the same question that you just did. Their journey might help you find your answer.'

King Sikhidhwaja and Queen Kundala were not only rulers but also spiritual aspirants. They studied, reflected and discussed higher truths together. Over time, the queen's inner clarity deepened. She realized the Self through direct experience. She saw that the essence of her being was not limited to her role, her body or even her name.

One evening, the king noticed something different about her. 'You seem changed,' he said. 'What's the secret behind the glow in your heart?'

She answered simply. 'I've come to know that the truth we seek is already present. The Self is not elsewhere but has always been here within me.'

The king did not take her seriously. 'You speak in riddles,' he said. 'You are wise in your own way, but these are matters far beyond you.'

Kundala didn't argue. She allowed him to keep his views. But within her, the truth remained firm.

Meanwhile, Sikhidhwaja grew restless. He began to feel that palace life was a distraction. He believed that in order to find peace, he needed to renounce everything. One day, without informing anyone, he left the kingdom. He gave away his wealth, removed his royal clothing and walked into the forest.

He lived alone, ate little and sat for long hours in meditation, but peace did not come. He still thought about what he had left behind. His doubts, pride and frustration stirred inside him. Nothing outside him was distracting him, yet his inner world was full of noise.

When Queen Kundala came to know of this, she understood that he had gone to find peace, but his attachments were holding him down. She also knew that if she tried to explain it, he would not listen. So she used magic and disguised herself as a young Brahmin boy named Kumbha and found the king in the forest. Kumbha said, 'O Great Seeker, I see you're walking the path. May I join you on your quest?'

The king was sceptical at first, but he liked the boy, so he allowed him to stay.

Over time, Kumbha began to teach him through everyday conversations. He shared gentle nudges of wisdom like, 'Renunciation isn't about giving up things. It's about giving up your craving for them.' 'Peace doesn't come from running away. It comes from seeing clearly,' among others.

The king began to listen, and slowly his pride vanished.

Now, Kumbha tested him. A celestial being appeared, offering him a trip to heaven, full of pleasures and freedom from pain. Sikhidhwaja declined, saying, 'True peace isn't in pleasures. It's in stillness.'

One by one, his illusions left him. His anger cooled, his pride waned and his need to be right gave way to understanding.

Finally, one day, Kumbha revealed the truth.

'I am Kundala,' she said, dropping the disguise. 'I am your wife, who never left you. I only changed my form to be with you.'

The king was stunned. His eyes filled with tears. 'You've been my teacher all along.'

They returned to their kingdom and lived with wisdom, detachment and love. They ruled with clarity. In time, they both attained complete liberation.

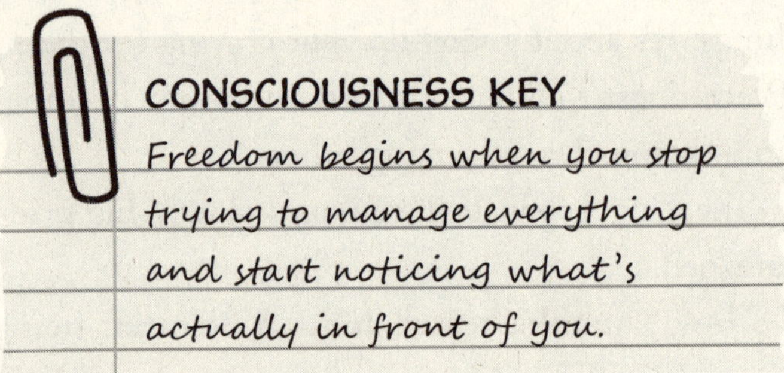

When the story ended, I sat silently beside my teacher. It was clear to me now that the outer act of leaving something is not the same as freedom from it. Real detachment isn't rejection, rather the absence of need to control or possess. You can care and still not be attached. You can be fully present while being inwardly free.

TRY THIS IN REAL LIFE

Relatable Situation

You are involved in a close relationship or an important responsibility. You want to give your best, but you notice you feel restless or irritated when things don't go your way. You expect certain responses, and when they don't come, it affects how you think and act.

What To Do

From Appendix 12, do the technique that helps create cheerful acceptance of any outcome whatsoever.

Why This Helps

When you expect people or situations to match your idea of how they should be, it creates tension. This practice helps you step back and accept things as they are.

11

Create Because It's Your Nature

I, Ram, was supposed to be paying attention to myself. But my soul was floating somewhere outside the solar system. Vasishtha had told me that enlightenment doesn't mean escaping the world but being free in it. But now, I had bigger questions: If everything is an illusion, if the world dissolves, if creation ends at the close of every *kalpa* (a day of Brahma, lasting 4.32 billion human years), then why does it all start again? And why would Brahma, the Creator, repeat the same cosmic performance day after day? Would he not get tired?

Later, I met Sage Vasishtha. He took one look at me and chuckled. 'Very good. These questions in your mind indicate that your mind is evolving.'

He placed a hand on my shoulder. 'Would it

surprise you to know that Brahma himself once asked the same thing? Let me tell you a story.'

Vasishtha began by telling me that when Brahma sleeps, all of creation returns into him. So when the Creator finally woke up after a long night, he stretched and got ready to begin his work of creation. But then he suddenly stopped in confusion. Because in the silence of the cosmic morning, he saw something strange.

He saw ten Brahmas.

Each of them was sitting on a lotus and creating their own universes as if it were just another Monday. Each was looking serene and swan-like. The original Brahma was confused, and rightfully so. 'What is *this*?' he muttered. 'Who are *they*? I thought I was the only Brahma in this universe.'

He asked Surya, the sun god, 'Enlighten me as to who these other Brahmas are and where they came from.'

Surya replied, 'Let me tell you a story from the previous kalpa.

'Long ago, in the Himalayas near Mount Kailash, lived a sage named Indu, a descendant of the great Kashyapa. He and his wife were childless for many years. So they climbed the mountain and went into meditation and prayer.

Eventually, Lord Shiva appeared. "Ask for any boon," he said.

The couple asked for ten sons, intelligent, radiant and spiritually elevated. Ten brilliant sons were born who were profound thinkers. They asked questions like *"Why do we suffer?"*, *"What is death?"* and *"What is the source of all power?"*.

The parents died when the boys were still young, and the loss hit them deeply. But rather than staying in their sorrow, the brothers chose to follow in their parents' footsteps and climb Mount Kailash to seek answers.

They began discussing the various roles in the universe: Kings. Emperors. Gods. Even the king of gods.

Then the eldest brother said, "Every role and form comes and goes. But Brahma, the Creator, remains through the entire kalpa. He lasts the longest and endures everything."

The others nodded. "Then tell us, dear brother, how do we become like Brahma?"

"Simple," he said, "Close your eyes and meditate on your heart. Imagine yourselves as Brahma and dissolve everything into that awareness."

The ten brothers meditated so intensely, so purely, that their bodies dissolved into light and their sense of individuality vanished. They entered *samadhi*, a trance so deep that they became one with the Creative Source.

So powerful was their meditation that they literally manifested ten orbs of consciousness. Each orb became a new Brahma, and each created a new universe. Thus, the ten Brahmas created themselves through pure identification with the Supreme Creator. That's the power of pure consciousness.'

Brahma frowned. 'Then is there any point in *my* creating anything at all? Haven't they already done the job?'

Now Surya smiled. 'Your creation is not a task but an act of love. You do not create because you must but because it is your nature to give.'

And then he added something profound, 'If you stop creating out of envy or doubt, what good is your vast capacity? A dusty mirror reflects nothing. But when cleaned, it shows the light.'

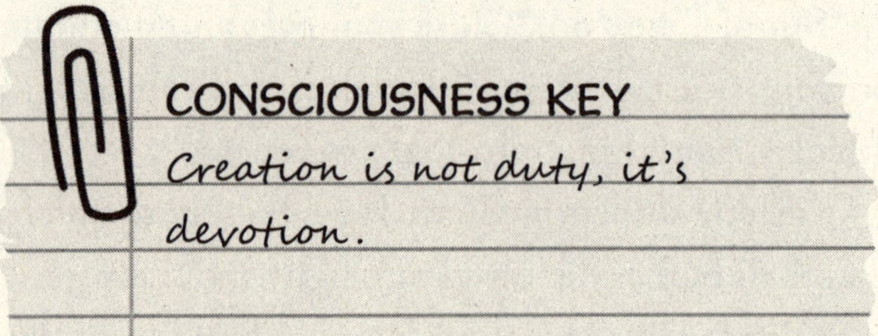

So Brahma got up, let go of his doubt and returned to his work, shaping galaxies, stars and souls. He created with joy, with purpose and without pressure. The ten Brahmas created too, each in his own way. Because the universe isn't a competition. It's a shared expression of consciousness.

TRY THIS IN REAL LIFE

Relatable Situation

You want to create something, like write a poem, compose a tune, paint or speak, but you keep holding back. You're afraid it won't be good enough, or that others might not get it. So you delay, hesitate or overthink.

What To Do

Before starting, sit for a moment in silence. As explained in Appendix 13, practice Constant Remembrance and connect yourself to the deepest core of your heart before beginning any activity. Now, begin your creative work from that connection.

Why This Helps

When you act from your heart, there is no fear of judgement. This practice connects you to the place where real inspiration lives, which is beyond approval, beyond fear, hope and beyond even yourself.

Gate 2

Peaceful Self-Control

12

Carried Away by a Single Desire

Vasishtha turned to me one morning and said, 'Ram, there are worlds beyond where we live. But not all of them are outside us. Some are inside, imagined so vividly that we forget they aren't real.'

Then he told me the story of Shukra.

Shukra was the only son of the great Sage Bhrigu. Like his father, he meditated for hours beneath a stony ridge above a lush garden. From that stillness, his mind became vast and luminous. One day, while gazing down at the garden, he saw a celestial nymph glide through the air, glowing like starlight.

Though he was attracted to her, he resumed his meditation. Outwardly, he sat like a sage, but inwardly, something happened.

In his imagination, he chased the nymph into

CONSCIOUSNESS KEY

Desire doesn't always shout. Sometimes, it whispers its way into the silence.

the heavens. He saw himself welcomed by gods, praised by Indra, given palaces of music and dance and revelled in divine romance. In this inner theatre, he lived with her through many lifetimes as a priest, a warrior, a king, a hermit. In some lives, he died in battle and in others, he died alone. In one, he was reborn as a deer. In another, he was a wandering monk. He saw joys, losses, rebirths and death after death.

But none of it actually happened in reality.

He was still under the rock and yet, within, he had spun the wheel of imagination. The stories felt so real that his body stopped functioning and he slipped into a yogic death.

When Sage Bhrigu noticed his son hadn't returned, he used his inner vision to search for him. He found Shukra's lifeless body near the river, untouched by any beast or insect, preserved by the intensity of his penance. He cried out in grief, called on the god of death and, in his anguish, prepared to curse him.

But the god of death stood calmly and said, 'Great Sage, you know that those who are born must die. Why be angry at the cycle that you yourself taught others to transcend?'

Bhrigu asked, 'How did my son die in meditation?'

The god of death smiled. 'He didn't die. He got lost in his own mind. Within a single breath, he imagined thousands of lives, and his mind went on a journey his body couldn't contain.'

Then he said, 'Look into his mind.'

Bhrigu closed his eyes and entered the subtle field of Shukra's thoughts. There he saw them all, the fantasies, the desires, the rewards, the rise, the fall. All of them were imagined and self-created.

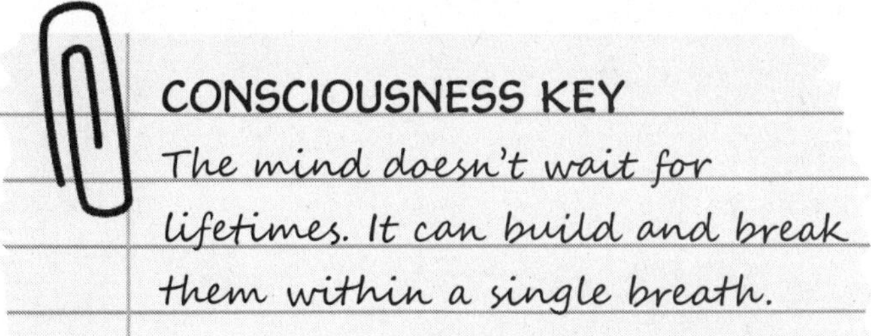

The god of death said, 'This is what happens to many, even while alive. They carry sorrow from imagined futures and joy from illusions. But beyond all that is the real Self, untouched by dream or memory.'

With that, he gently touched Shukra's head. Breath returned to the boy's body and his eyelids fluttered open.

Years later, Shukra became a teacher to many, even to the asuras. Some say he became the very spirit of the planet Venus.

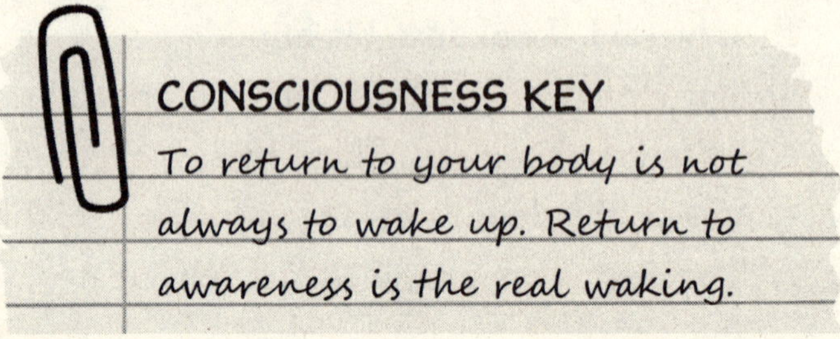

TRY THIS IN REAL LIFE

Relatable Situation

You're obsessed with one goal – getting into a dream college, winning a competition or getting selected for something important. It fills your thoughts day and night. You imagine it constantly and panic when it seems far.

What To Do

Take ten quiet minutes with a notebook. Use a combination of Appendices 7, 8 or/and 9. First do guided inquiry and ask yourself questions like:

- What do I believe this achievement will give me?
- What am I afraid of if I don't get it?
- Where else have I found that same feeling before?

Continue doing left-nostril breathing technique and limb cleaning technique to get your balance back.

Why This Helps

Obsession leads to fear of failure, rejection or not being enough. However inquiry reveals the real need behind the goal and frees you from being consumed by it.

13

What You Build Is Not Who You Are

One evening, I asked Vasishtha, 'If everything we hold on to, like our names, our bodies, our roles, is just temporary, then who are we really? And what are we holding onto so tightly?'

He replied, 'Ram, let me tell you about a man who was floating in space.'

He went on to narrate the tale of this man, who was just suspended in an infinite silence, untouched by time or place. He had no family, no memory, no past. He called himself the Aerial Man. He didn't know how he got there. He was alone in the vastness of space.

One day, he decided to build himself a home. A floating hut on the side of his space shuttle that he could claim as his own. He imagined it clearly: a chamber harnessing solar energy, capturing air. And for a while, he was content.

But then the winds of space howled and asteroids struck. His little chamber shattered. He wept and mourned his loss.

'I had a place,' he cried, 'and now it's gone.'

So he built it again. He built a tub, and then a cave and then a domed capsule of light. Each time there was destruction, followed by despair. He grieved the loss of each structure as if it were his soul. But they were all just shapes in shapeless space.

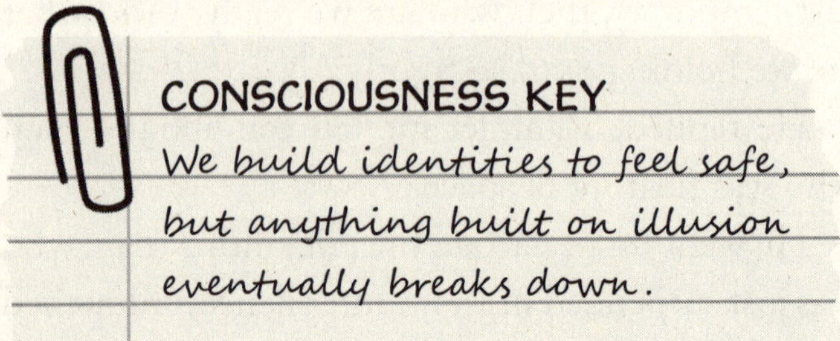

When I asked Vasishtha what this meant, he said, 'Ram, the Aerial Man is all of us. We build names, roles, beliefs, and call them "I", while floating in the vast space of consciousness. But these are temporary structures, held together by imagination and ego. When life takes them away, as it always does, we grieve the loss of something that was never truly solid.'

He looked at me with gentleness. 'The man wasn't crying at the loss of a home but over the idea that he had something to lose.'

The Aerial man mourned the loss of each form, not realizing that what he was trying to protect wasn't real to begin with. It was just a temporary idea of himself, not who he truly was.

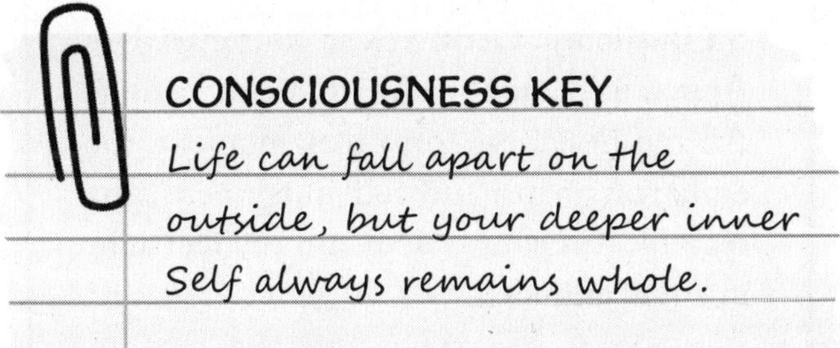

His story is the story of every soul passing through lifetimes, one body, one personality, one storyline after another.

TRY THIS IN REAL LIFE

Relatable Situation

Suppose you failed in front of others, like you didn't make the team, forgot your lines, lost a debate or just had a moment that felt humiliating, and now your mind keeps replaying it and your heart feels heavy whenever you think about it.

What To Do

Sit in silence. Gently close your eyes. Use Appendix 3 and the Heartfulness cleaning. All the heaviness from that moment, the embarrassment, the self-judgement, the regret leaves your system and you feel light in a few minutes.

Why This Helps

When you confuse any role or any failure or any success with your actual identity, you start feeling heavy and restless. This practice helps you clean that inner impression, so that you can continue to learn, evolve and become more whole.

14

The Effort to Let Go Is the First Freedom

One morning, after my meditation, I asked Vasishtha, 'Why is it that even when I let go of something – a desire, a possession, a plan – it still lingers in my mind? I let go, but I don't feel free.'

He smiled and said, 'Ram, letting go is not an act of the hand, it is an act of the mind. Listen to the story of Kacha, the son of Brihaspati.'

Brihaspati, the guru of the gods, had a son named Kacha. As a young man, Kacha was sincere, curious and troubled by the suffering he saw around him and inside him.

He went to his father and asked, 'How can I overcome the constant worries of life, this inner heaviness, confusion and searching?'

His father said simply, 'Let go.'

Kacha took the words literally. He gave away all his possessions, renounced comfort and lived in silence. He meditated under trees and stars but the peace he expected never came. The worry was still there.

He came back to his father.

'I gave up everything,' he said. 'Why do I still feel burdened?'

Brihaspati replied, 'Peace doesn't come from what you give up on the outside. It depends on how your mind relates to what's happening. If you understand that, even a noisy place can feel calm. If you don't, even the quietest place will make you feel restless.'

So Kacha returned again, this time to observe his mind directly. He tried to control it, correct it and force it to be still. But it did not work.

CONSCIOUSNESS KEY

Letting go of the world will not work if you're still holding on to yourself.

He returned to his father again. 'I've tried to master the mind, but I can't control it.'

His father nodded. 'That's because the root isn't just desire, it's also identity. As long as you think, "I'm the one who has to succeed, stay peaceful or become enlightened," the ego is still in control.'

Kacha asked, 'Then how do I give up ego?'

Brihaspati smiled and said, 'You don't remove it by force but see through it. Meditate on the oneness that is present in everything, and understand that there is no real division between "I" and "they", or "mine" and "yours". When the sense of separation fades, ego no longer has anything to hold on to, and it falls away on its own, like a shadow at sunset.'

So Kacha sat down in meditation again. He did not try to control anything but merely witnessed what was happening in his mind.

Gradually, his thoughts began to settle down. His mind became quieter and he could see what mattered. He felt a simplicity and naturalness in his meditation.

CONSCIOUSNESS KEY

The mind works best when you're not caught up in proving or protecting yourself.

TRY THIS IN REAL LIFE

Relatable Situation

Someone you cared about, like a best friend or significant other, suddenly stopped communicating. They no longer respond to your messages or make time for you. You don't know why, and there has been no conversation to explain the change. You feel unsettled and distracted, unsure how to act or what to think.

What To Do

Close your eyes and remember the second suggestion from Appendix 11 of the Prayerful

Suggestions. When everyone develops correct thinking, right understanding and an honest approach to life, there will be purity in thought and action.

Why This Helps

Ghosting traps your energy in waiting. When someone stops responding, the mind circles around what went wrong. Kacha's story shows that letting go begins when we stop controlling the story. This prayer brings the mind back to clarity and encourages a clear way forward.

15

Doubt Can Undo Everything

One day, I asked Vasishtha, 'Why do some people work so hard, chase something for years and then, just when it's in front of them, hesitate and walk away?'

He replied, 'Ram, not every failure is due to lack of effort. Some come from doubt. When doubt is disguised as caution, it can be more dangerous than ignorance.'

Then he told me a story of a wealthy merchant who was smart, strategic and successful in every way except one. He had no faith in anything beyond his own calculations.

One day, he heard of the philosopher's stone that could turn anything into gold. He wanted this treasure of unimaginable value. He worked for years to find it. He tried to bribe sages, studied secrets, travelled through deserts and mountains. And finally he found it after a lot of effort. As it lay in front of him, glowing and radiant, he froze.

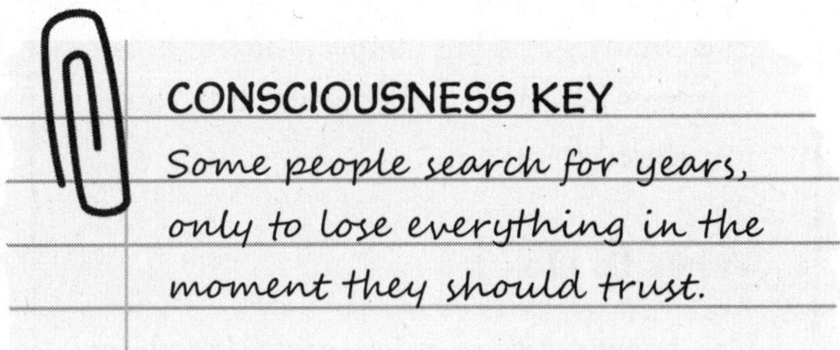

'What if it's not real?' he thought. 'What if I touch it and it disappears? What if it's cursed? What if it's too good to be true?'

He hesitated and waited too long, and the stone disappeared. Later, he found a shiny piece of glass that was a worthless, brittle, flashy fragment resembling the stone.

He convinced himself, 'Maybe this is real and it just looks different.'

He gave away his wealth, bet everything on that glass and carried it into the world. But this was not the philosopher's stone. The glass was never magic.

TRY THIS IN REAL LIFE

Relatable Situation

You finally got a big chance, the big break that you had been aspiring for, but you're too scared to take it.

What To Do

Use Appendix 8 and do left-nostril breathing for five to seven minutes before the event.

Why This Helps

This calms nervous anticipation and helps centre your action.

16

Desire Rehearsed Is Destiny Chosen

Vasishtha once told me, 'Ram, the mind can make anything beautiful, even what is destructive. And when that imagined beauty becomes an obsession, it can blur every boundary.'

Then he told me about Queen Ahalya. Let's call her Ahalya 1 for now.

One day, Ahalya 1 overheard the story of another Ahalya, who was a sage's wife. Let's call her Ahalya 2. She had been deceived by the god Indra. In that story, Indra had disguised himself as the sage and visited his wife, Ahalya 2, who unknowingly accepted him. When the truth came out, the sage cursed her, and she was turned into stone.

Now Ahalya 1 became fascinated. She thought, *'How exciting it must have been to dance and fly and have a good time with a god like Indra.'*

She imagined it again and again, and her mind began to craft a world around her infatuated fantasy. Now she wanted her fantasy to become real. In her own city, she heard of a man named Indra, who was charismatic, charming and surrounded by women. Though he was not a god, he was available.

She sent for him.

They met in secret. They danced, wandered through gardens, and the queen, who was once a pillar of dignity, let herself be carried away.

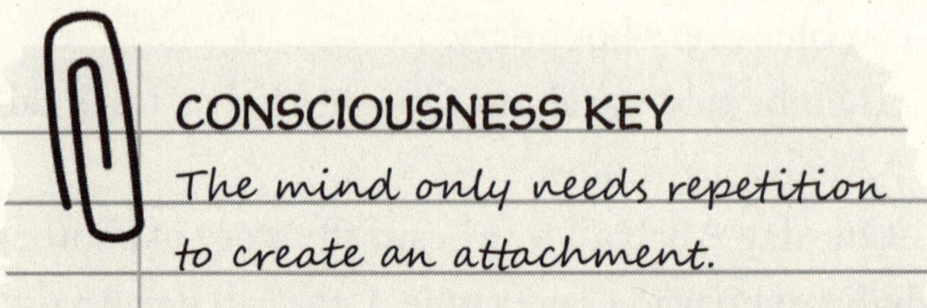

When the king found out, he was heartbroken.

He said to her calmly, 'Ahalya 2 was deceived by Indra as Indra disguised himself as her husband. Her mistake was innocent, but yours is deliberate. How do you think God's grace will reach you?'

But it was too late. Ahalya 1's imagination had shaped her path, and the man named Indra had shaped his fantasy too, believing himself to be divine and deserving of the same story.

When Sage Bharat heard of it, he saw through the self-deception. He cursed them both and they died instantly. But they were not released from their bondage of karma.

They were born again as a pair of deer. Even in animal form, their attraction was strong. Then they were reborn as turtle doves, and then as foxes and then much later as humans again.

In each life, they met again, and in each life their pull was strong.

Eventually, after countless births, they were awakened to spiritual life. The attachment that was once sweet now felt hollow. So they turned inwards and meditated. Finally, they were freed, from each other and from themselves.

Vasishtha said, 'Ram, the mind is not just a mirror. It's also a painter. If you give it the same thought often enough, it will start to live inside that thought.'

I understood what he meant. This was a story about obsession and how fantasy, when fed, becomes karma.

TRY THIS IN REAL LIFE

Relatable Situation

You can't stop imagining being with someone – a crush, an ex or someone who isn't emotionally available. You build scenarios in your head. You imagine conversations, closeness, futures. But none of it is happening, except inside you.

What To Do

Use Appendix 7 and do guided inquiry. Open your journal and write your answers to these questions:

- What exactly am I imagining will happen with this person?
- What feeling am I chasing through that fantasy? Is it love, safety, validation, excitement?
- Have I ever felt that same feeling elsewhere, in a real and grounded way?

Why This Helps

Fantasy can hijack your attention and identity. This practice brings you back to your real life, your own heart, your own emotional truth, so that you can stop chasing what isn't there and begin to see what already is.

17

The Poise That Outlasted the World

On the northern side of Mount Meru, there lived an ancient crow named Kaka Bhushunda. But he was also a sage who was ageless, deathless and serene.

When Vasishtha heard about him from an old sage named Salatapa, he set out to meet him. I, too, had heard of Bhushunda before, and I was filled with curiosity.

At the summit, Vasishtha found him cloaked in stillness. Around him were flocks of birds: swans, peacocks, cranes, parrots, storks, pelicans and many rows of crows. But in the centre of it all, on a perch near a kalpa tree, sat Bhushunda. His feathers shimmered blue-black like moonlit ink and his eyes were deep with silence. He greeted Vasishtha warmly.

'Please tell me your story,' Vasishtha asked.

Bhushunda told of ancient sages like Shiva, Brahmi and Alampusha, and of a great crow named Chanda, who married seven swan-mothers. From their union, twenty-one crow-sons were born who were full of wisdom. They were raised in devotion, and Bhushunda was one of them.

The young crows learnt everything from scripture to skills and stillness. But they longed for stillness and silence. So their father sent them to meditate at the kalpa tree. One by one, they discovered their Selves and the changeless presence within.

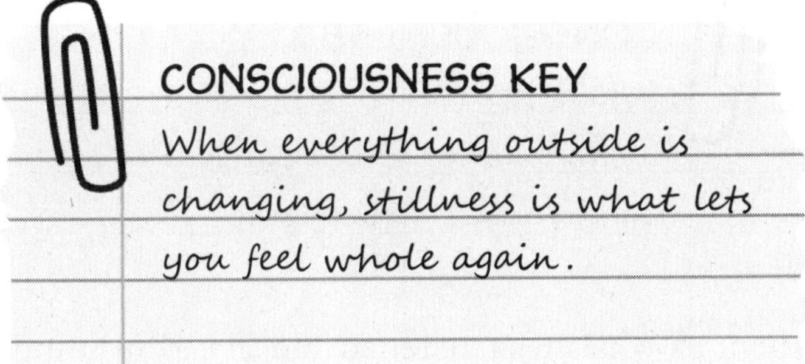

But with time, all his brothers passed away. Civilizations rose and fell, floods washed away the earth and even the skies disappeared. But Bhushunda remained, hovering in space, bodyless in samadhi. And when the world was created again, he returned to the kalpa tree.

Bhushunda told Vasishtha, 'The tree is here because I want it to be here. When there is no north, no south, no form, no time, I remain as pure awareness.'

Vasishtha then asked, 'What is the secret of your peace? How do you stay unaffected by death?'

Bhushunda replied, 'Death cannot approach the one who has no fire of desires burning in the heart. I have no anger, no greed, and no envy. And above all, I place complete faith in the Supreme Self.'

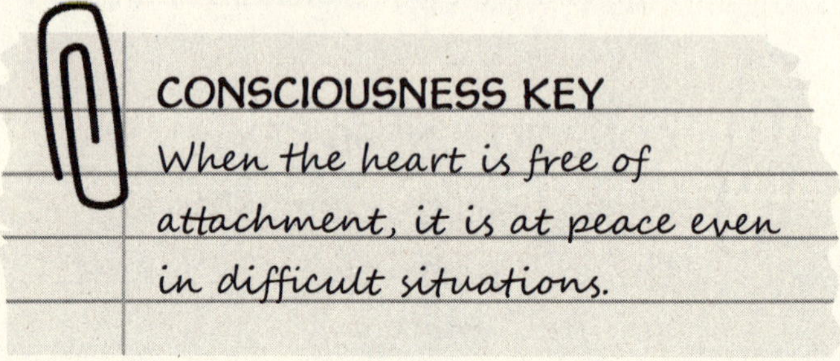

Then, as Vasishtha listened closely, Bhushunda taught him his simple path:

- To sit under the kalpa tree.
- To watch the breath rise and fall.

- To stay present with every inhale, every pause, every exhale.
- To never abandon this even if the mountain shakes.

He explained the five movements of vital energy: *prana*, *apana*, *vyana*, *samana* and *udana*. He showed Vasishtha how breath, when observed with reverence, becomes the gateway to eternal calm.

When the lesson was complete, Vasishtha bowed and said, 'In all my journeys, I've met many sages, but none like you. You have conquered time.'

Bhushunda gave him a flower from the kalpa tree and a pearl of pure brightness from his own beak. Vasishtha returned home, where his wise wife Arundhati welcomed him.

As I listened intently to Vasishtha's tale, I asked, 'If the body dreams of going to distant worlds while lying still, where is the real me?'

Vasishtha smiled and answered, 'The body is not the Self. Your real home is in the unmoving consciousness. Keep yourself close to that, and let go of all the rest.'

TRY THIS IN REAL LIFE

Relatable Situation

When you feel overwhelmed by constant uncertainty from news, face school pressure or changing plans, or want peace but don't know where to find it, do the below-mentioned practice.

What To Do

Sit comfortably and gently close your eyes. From Appendix 11, do prayerful suggestion of everything surrounding us being deeply absorbed in godly remembrance. Slowly bring your attention to your heart and think that the source of light within your heart is attracting you inwards.

Why This Helps

This practice helps you shift your attention from external noise to something pure and poised within. This practice helps you reduce your feeling of overwhelm and helps you return to the centre of your being.

18

Renunciation Is Inside the Action

I once asked my teacher Vasishtha, 'How can we act in this world without getting stuck, without fear, without being attached and without regret?'

He answered with a story from long ago.

The king of a simple mountain tribe, the Bhringis, once asked Shiva a question full of desperation. 'This world is broken and there is so much sorrow. What is just that one truth that we can hold onto that will not collapse?'

Shiva's reply was both simple and vast: 'Rely on your patience and renounce all else. And do your best in whatever you do, with passion and clarity.'

The Bhringi king was wise, and wanted more.

'What does it mean to act well, to enjoy well and to renounce well?'

Shiva answered, 'The best actor is one who acts without expectation or fear, without attachment or anxiety, without ego, anger or envy. He acts when the time is right, and is silent when it isn't.'

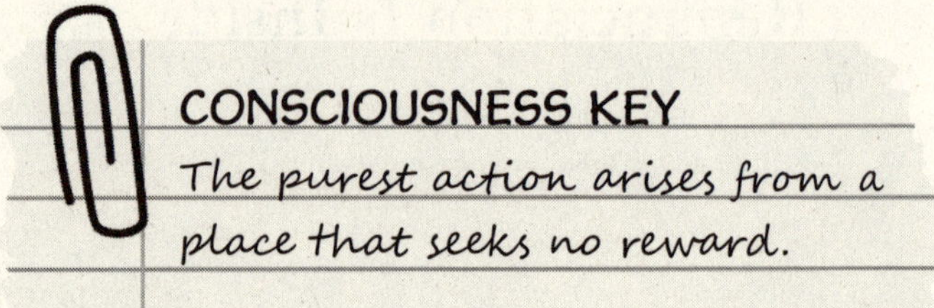

'The best enjoyer is he who envies no one. He cheerfully accepts whatever happens and enjoys without being attached. He's not affected by pain or inflated by joy. He welcomes good fortune with balance and misfortune with peace.

The best renouncer is one who doesn't run away from life. He lets go of desire, fear and hope, and is not affected by the senses or the moods of the mind. The real sacrifice is not giving up things, but giving up attachment.'

When Vasishtha finished the story, he looked at me and said, 'Ram, this is how you must live. Meditate on the eternal spirit and let go of the idea that anything outside can give you lasting happiness. Let your actions be done such that your identity is separate from it. Then you will live in joy.'

TRY THIS IN REAL LIFE

Relatable Situation

You're trying to do the right thing, like study, show up, help others, but there's a heaviness inside. You don't know why it feels so tiring, like something old is weighing you down.

What To Do

Sit comfortably and close your eyes. Do guided limb cleaning from Appendix 9. Your emotional burdens melt away.

Why This Helps

This practice clears emotional residues and deep impressions (*vasana*s) that may influence your choices. Just like Shiva taught, true action is free from hidden fear. This practice helps clear those roots.

19

Your Inner Impressions Shape the Next Life

Vasishtha once told me about a king named Prajnapti, who ruled the distant island of Kusha-Dwipa. King Prajnapti was also a seeker. One day, he came to Vasishtha and asked, 'When the world is fully destroyed during the great cosmic dissolution, how is it rebuilt? Is everything destroyed or just some parts? And where does the material for rebuilding the world come from?'

Then he leant closer and asked what I too have secretly wondered: 'How can something immaterial, like a soul or pure consciousness, give rise to a material world?'

Vasishtha's reply was strange at first, 'The world seems to exist, like a dream seems real while you're in it. But when you wake up, you see that there was nothing there at all. This world is like that. It appears, but it is not ultimately real. The only thing that truly exists is supreme consciousness, and all forms are its reflections.'

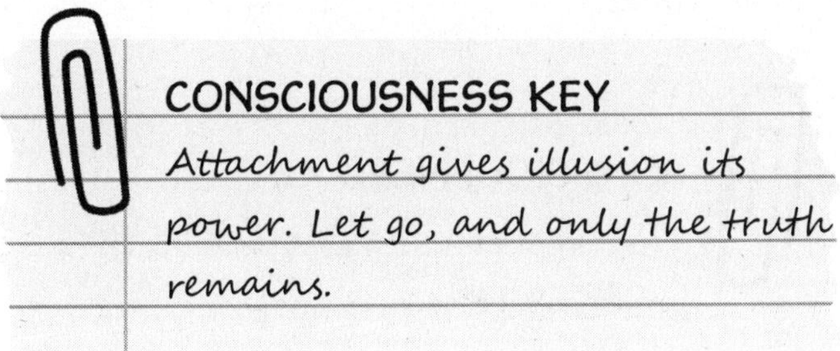

Still, King Prajnapti wanted more clarity. 'If everything is temporary and only appears to exist,' he asked, 'then what's the point of action? Why do scriptures say that charity or piety give rewards in the next life? What good is that reward to the body I have *now*? Won't the soul have moved on?'

Vasishtha answered, 'Does a dead body feel anything? No. Because consciousness belongs to the soul, not to the body. And that soul continues to live in rebirth. Even in this life, when you act kindly or selfishly, what is it that feels joy or pain? It is the soul. And it's *that* feeling of joy or pain that is carried forward in the next birth.'

Then he continued, 'If you want to know what is permanent, look for what does not change. Is it the objects? Or is it the *feeling*? Or the *idea?* What is the impression that remains with you far longer than anything?'

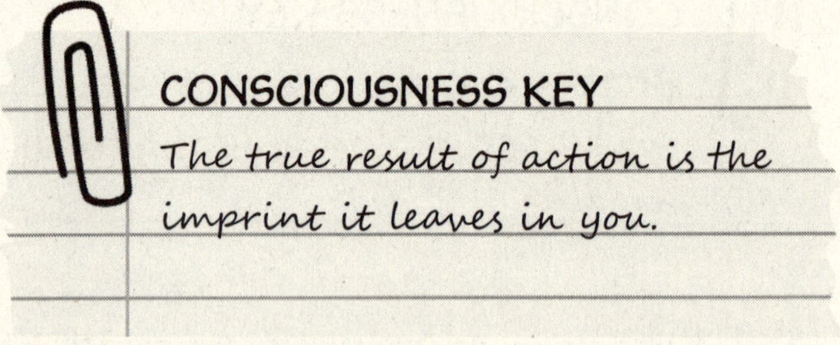

Vasishtha told me that it is our residue of feeling that recreates our experience again and again, even in new bodies. And the way out is to act without ego, to live with awareness and to let go of the attachment that keeps pulling us back.

TRY THIS IN REAL LIFE

Relatable Situation

You're realizing that your habits – binge-watching, negative self-talk, overthinking – are returning to shape your moods and days.

What To Do

Write down three qualities you deeply admire (e.g., kindness, clarity, courage). For each one, write: 'How am I already practicing this?' and 'Where can I bring this more into my week?'

Why This Helps

This links your daily choices with the person you want to become. Your conscious awareness of your aspirations is the first step towards letting go of unwanted qualities.

20

From Pure Light to Form, and the Way Back

Vasishtha told me a story that shattered the way I think of identity. He started by telling me, 'Ram, pure consciousness does not stay still. When it begins to identify with thought, it creates form, like water falling into shapes made of clay. That is how creation begins and that is how the Self forgets its source.'

He told me of a wandering mendicant who was meditating and his trance dissolved every impurity. When he emerged from his meditation, he decided to contemplate the condition of an ordinary man named Jivata. The moment he thought of Jivata, he *became* Jivata. Jivata dreamt he was a Brahmin performing rituals. So he *became* a Brahmin. That

Brahmin dreamt of being a Kshatriya chieftain. He became the chieftain. The chieftain dreamt of being a king. And so on.

Each dream gave rise to the next. The king dreamt he was a heavenly woman. The woman dreamt she was a deer. The deer dreamt it was a plant. The plant dreamt it was a tree. The tree dreamt it was a bee. The bee was crushed under an elephant's foot and dreamt that it became an elephant. The elephant finally dreamt that it became a swan, and the swan, seeing the mighty Rudra meditating, wanted to become Rudra.

And so it did.

Now this new Rudra, full of power, returned to the mendicant's body and gave it life. They both went back, reviving each former form one by one, until there were a 100 Rudras all present at once.

The first Rudra looked at all the others and whispered, 'How strange. I was once only pure light. And by imagining form, I became mind ... then body ... then a hundred different lives.'

Vasishtha told me they all lived out their lives as reflections of that first Rudra, and eventually merged back into supreme consciousness.

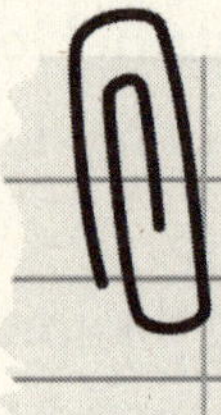

CONSCIOUSNESS KEY

You're not the thoughts or feelings that come and go. You're the one who notices them.

Then I asked him a new question. 'There are many kinds of silence, aren't there? The silence of the mouth, the silence of the senses, the silence which is like deep sleep, and so on. I don't understand them all.'

Vasishtha nodded. 'The silence of the ascetic who forces stillness is like the muteness of a wooden idol. But the silence of the liberated soul is true. He walks through the world with no fear, no longing, and no disturbance inside him.'

CONSCIOUSNESS KEY

You don't have to look for silence. It's there when you stop managing, performing and proving.

TRY THIS IN REAL LIFE

Relatable Situation

You feel cluttered and mentally foggy. You feel unclear about your direction. You don't know what you want or who you are becoming.

What To Do

Sit comfortably and gently close your eyes. Try the Heartfulness meditation as given in Appendix 2. Suppose that the source of divine light is present in your heart and it is drawing you inwards. Remain with that feeling. If your attention drifts, gently return to your heart. Meditate for fifteen to twenty minutes.

Why This Helps

An everyday practice of meditation helps you reconnect with your heart. This links a daily action with intentional clarity.

Gate 3

Discrimination Through Inquiry

21

The Mind That Dreamt a Lifetime

I remember clearly the day I asked Vasishtha, 'Gurudev, how is it that the world feels so real, and yet, so unreal the moment I close my eyes in meditation? How can something so vivid dissolve so easily? Is the world an illusion or am I the illusion?'

Vasishtha didn't answer right away. Then he said, 'Ram, the world is not what it appears to be. It is an enchanted city, conjured by the magician called "mind". Let me tell you how powerful that magician really is.' He then shared the story of King Lavana.

Lavana was humble, generous and brave, the kind of ruler poets sing about and warriors die for. His court was radiant, his people loved him and, by all accounts, he had mastered the art of ruling.

One day, while Lavana was sitting in his court, something unusual happened. An illusionist arrived – an actual conjurer – requesting permission to perform. Before Lavana could respond, another messenger showed up, presenting a horse. The horse was a magnificent creature that shimmered like a comet and stood with divine pride. The illusionist, already twirling his wand, sent spirals of light flickering through the air. The entire court fell silent and Lavana's eyes locked onto the horse.

'Ride it, O King!' said the magician. 'Let your joy soar like the sun!'

Lavana was captivated. He mounted the horse, closed his eyes and went completely still. He did not blink and it was as though someone had hit pause on reality. The courtiers panicked. Their king, just moments ago the centre of the court, was now invisible from within. He was a body without awareness. Thus two hours passed.

And then, suddenly, the king shuddered as if an earthquake had passed through his soul.

The courtiers helped him down gently, placing him on his throne. His lips trembled. His eyes blinked. And then he looked around in pure confusion. 'Where am I?' he asked. 'Whose kingdom is this?'

Everyone stared. 'You are our king!' they cried. 'What spell took over you?'

One minister stepped forward. 'You are wise. You know better than anyone that pleasure is temporary and illusion leads to misery. But still you fell prey. Wake up, O King!'

The king took a deep breath. The colour returned to his face. His eyes cleared, like clouds rolling away from the full moon. And he whispered, 'Let me tell you what I saw.'

'When I stared at that horse,' he began, 'I saw a beautiful country. The court shimmered like a heaven I never knew existed. I mounted the horse and rode through an endless desert where the sun blazed. By nightfall, I had lost all sense of self. I found a forest and slept inside a hollow tree. I was hungry, lost and alone.'

His voice grew quieter. 'The next day, I met a tribal woman. She carried food and water. I begged her, please, just one bite. She said the food was for her father and the only way she would share it was if I became her husband.

I was starving. So I said yes.

She took me to her tribe of fierce and wild cannibals. And then came the famine. Life was not kind, and my youngest son cried for meat. I had nothing to give and so I told him to cut flesh from my thigh and feed himself and his siblings.

I was about to light my own funeral pyre when suddenly, I heard the cries of "Victory to King Lavana!" echoing around me. I opened my eyes, and I was here, in this court, on my throne.'

He looked up.

'It was a spell, like a dream, but I lived it every second.'

He turned to find the illusionist, but he had vanished.

One of the ministers said, 'This was not an ordinary magician. This was nature itself, showing us what life really is.'

CONSCIOUSNESS KEY

What we call reality is just a longer dream.

I sat there, stunned. The story felt very real. It wasn't just about a king and a spell, it was also about us and our desires and distractions.

Vasishtha said, 'Ram, the mind is a magician. It can stretch a second into a century. It can compress a lifetime into a breath. It can create paradise in hell, or hell in paradise.'

He quoted a line I've never forgotten since: 'The mind is its own place and in itself, can make heaven of hell or hell of heaven.' He told me that the line came from a poet in a faraway land who is going to come to the world, millennia later.

CONSCIOUSNESS KEY

Your world is shaped not by what is, but by how your mind sees it.

TRY THIS IN REAL LIFE

Relatable Situation

You've been stuck inside your own head, imagining problems, conflicts or successes that haven't happened.

What To Do

Go outside and find a place where you can see the open sky. Sit or lie down and look up. Don't let your thoughts lead your senses. Let the sky remind you that awareness doesn't change. After ten to fifteen minutes, observe your mind and heart. Continue if you think it will help you more.

When your mind has spun a vivid story, a worry, a fear or a fantasy that feels real, you can clear it out of your system in this way. Then do the limb cleaning technique mentioned in Appendix 9.

Why This Helps

The sky gazing practice gives your system time and space to settle down. It helps you experience the difference between what is permanent and what is not. Later, the limb cleaning technique clears emotional residues left behind by intense or imaginary experiences. It helps restore clarity and reconnect you to the present.

22

You Are Not the Role You Wake Up In

One day, I asked Vasishtha, 'What if everything – this palace, these people, my life – is part of some giant, cosmic dream? What if I'm sleeping somewhere else, and this is just one flicker in a long, never-ending night?'

He replied, 'Ram, let me tell you the story of Gadhi, the man who dreamt an entire life, or perhaps lived a dream.'

Gadhi, a Brahmin by birth, was rooted in ritual, tradition and discipline. One morning, as part of his daily rites, he entered a serene lake to take his ritual bath. The water was cool, and as he dipped his head beneath the surface, he lost consciousness. It was then that he saw something.

First, he saw his own death and his relatives were crying at his funeral. Then he saw darkness, and later light.

He found himself inside a womb, hearing muffled tribal chants and forest sounds – he was a child in the belly of an outcast woman. Born into the wilderness, he grew up among tribals and became a hunter. He ate meat and took pride in killing. He fought with his clan, married and had children, and later became a grandfather.

One day, weary and weathered, he wandered into the bustling kingdom of Kira. And as fate would have it, the royal elephant was on a sacred mission to choose the next king. Adorned with garlands, glowing with divine instinct, the elephant walked through crowds until it paused in front of Gadhi and placed the garland around his neck.

Gadhi was stunned as the city erupted in celebration. He was taken to the palace, bathed, robed and crowned. He ruled for eight glorious years. The people loved him as he brought peace, justice and prosperity.

One day, an old tribal man recognized him. Whispers turned into rumours and rumours turned into revolt.

'Our king is from *where*? Is he a tribal? Is he an outcast?'

The court fell apart. Priests, nobles and ministers were disgusted, ashamed and horrified. They began to end their lives, one after another. Gadhi, shattered by guilt, stood on the funeral pyre, unable to live with the suffering he'd unknowingly caused.

CONSCIOUSNESS KEY

A dream can feel like a life. And a life can vanish like a dream. But the Self remains, untouched by both.

He stepped into the fire, and then he woke up. He was back in the lake and his body was still wet. The sun had barely moved, and it was as if no time had passed. He gasped, staggered out of the water, confused, dazed.

He told himself, '*It was only a strange, intense and terrifying dream.*'

And he let it go and returned to his normal life. He performed his rituals and lived peacefully as a priest.

Years later, an old traveller arrived at Gadhi's house. The man told a story about a kingdom named Kira, about a tribal king who ruled for eight years, about an elephant's garland, about an uprising and mass suicides, about the self-immolation of a king. Gadhi froze. He asked, 'What was the king's name?'

The old man told him the tribal name. It was the same name that Gadhi remembered from his dream. Chills ran down his spine. How could a dream be someone else's history?

He left his home and visited the tribal village. He found traces of his 'past' family. He found old records, testimonies – everything matched.

He went back three times. Again and again and again. And every time, he encountered the same result. It had happened, but he could not understand how. He had lived that life in a dream lasting only minutes. Yet in the world, it had spanned a century.

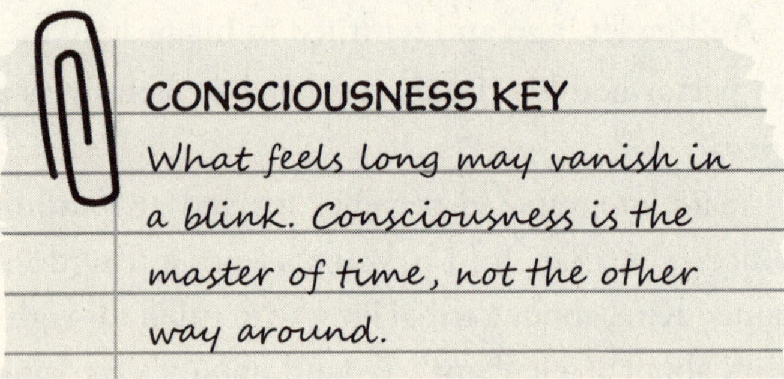

Gadhi fell to his knees. 'God,' he cried, 'what is real? Am I Gadhi? Or was I the tribal king? Or am I neither?'

And for the first time in his life, he heard an answer from within. 'Both the tribal king and the priest are dreams and flickers of imagination. Consciousness creates the stage. You are none of the roles, you are the one watching.'

When Vasishtha finished the story, I was more silent than usual. 'Gurudev,' I whispered, 'how do I know if my current life isn't a dream?'

'You don't,' he said. 'But the one asking that question, the Self inside you, that is the only real thing there is.'

TRY THIS IN REAL LIFE

Relatable Situation

You keep shifting roles – child, student, friend – and none feel like the real you. It's causing identity fatigue and anxiety. You're trying to be what others need, but deep down, you don't know what's actually you.

What To Do

Stand in front of a mirror. Look into your eyes. Not at your hairstyle, face or expression. Just your eyes. Ask yourself, 'Who is behind all of these roles?' Let that question settle down in your mind. Keep witnessing the few or many things that your mind comes up with. Let them come and go. Finally see what remains.

Now sit down and meditate for half an hour using the Heartfulness meditation technique as given in Appendix 2.

Why This Helps

This practice of standing in front of a mirror breaks the habit of relating to yourself through roles or surface images. It reminds you that you are not the personality you project. The practice of meditation allows the mind to go deeper into the Self and emerge with clarity. The roles we play rise and fall. But the witnessing presence, the inner Self, is unchanging.

23

The Source Is Already Within You

One afternoon, I asked Vasishtha, 'What is consciousness, really? Where does it begin? What shape does it have? Is it like a flame? A wind? An ocean?'

He didn't answer directly. Instead, he said, 'Ram, let me tell you a parable to help you feel this idea of consciousness rather than merely explaining it.'

He told me that in the centre of the universe, it is believed that there is a tree that continues to grow. This tree stretches across dimensions, its trunk spans galaxies, its roots anchor time, its branches cradle the stars. And on this tree grows the bael fruit, which is sweet and golden. The fruit is always ripe and beautiful, and it never rots.

Inside the bael fruit are infinite seeds, and inside each seed is an entire world. Just as a tree is hidden inside a seed, so too are lives, civilizations and dreams hidden inside these tiny orbs. Some say the spirit of God lives in the very core of that fruit.

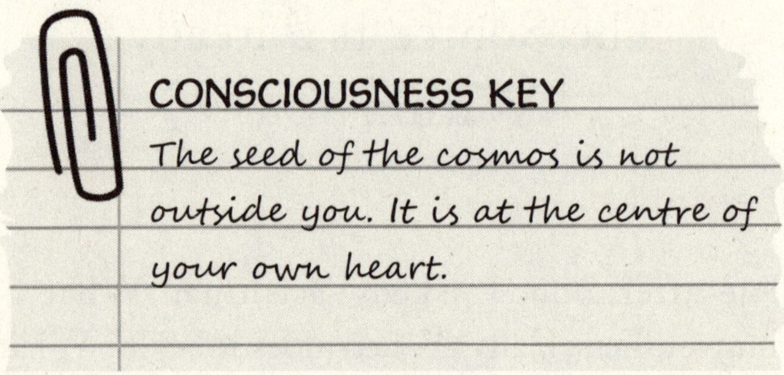

Vasishtha continued, 'Ram, this fruit is like your consciousness. The outer layers are your thoughts, emotions, identities. They may be sweet, bitter and changing.

'But at the centre is something still and pure. It is not your mind. It is not your personality. It is not even your idea of yourself.

'It is your essence. The place where all experience happens, but which itself is untouched by experience.'

He paused. 'But that is not all.'

He then spoke of another metaphor – the carved stone.

'Imagine,' he said, 'a massive radiant stone, shining like a star, uncut and untouched. Inside that stone are sleeping images of animals, forests, stars, waves, faces. They're not separate from the stone. They are the stone.

'Only when a sculptor chisels the surface do the figures emerge. But even then, they are still stone. So is the Self. All form, all identity, all differentiation is just a carving on the face of one consciousness.'

Vasishtha continued, 'Some worship the stone as sacred. But the true seeker goes beyond form, beyond idea, beyond even devotion.

'You are the one who existed before anyone gave you a name, before you were told who to be, and before you learnt to describe yourself in words.

'Just as the tree exists in the seed and the world within the fruit, you carry within you the entire cosmos.'

TRY THIS IN REAL LIFE

Relatable Situation

You've been searching hard, listening to podcasts, asking mentors, collecting advice, hoping someone will say the one thing that makes everything clear. But instead, you feel more overwhelmed and uncertain.

What To Do

Sit comfortably and gently close your eyes. Try the Heartfulness meditation as given in Appendix 2. Suppose that the source of divine light is present in your heart and it is drawing you inwards. Remain with that feeling. If your attention drifts, gently return to your heart. Meditate for fifteen to twenty minutes.

Why This Helps

Wisdom doesn't come from searching for more, it comes from turning inwards. This practice helps you experience the stillness where your clearest guidance already lives.

24

You Have to Want the Truth, Not Just the Tools

One morning, I caught myself doing something strange. I had spent an hour reading a scroll about truth, and the moment I finished, I reached for another and then another but not a word sunk in.

Vasishtha noticed and asked, 'Ram, you're carrying the entire forest of knowledge … but are you still just chopping wood?'

I did not understand, but he continued to explain, 'Words are only wood. They can keep a fire going, but they cannot light it.' And then he told me a story.

Once, there lived a group of poor woodcutters on the edge of a vast forest. They wore tattered clothes, barely ate enough to survive and spent each day chopping wood to earn a little money.

One day, they heard that deeper inside the forest were treasures like sandalwood trees, fruit-bearing groves, gold veins and even sparkling diamonds beneath the roots.

Some ignored the rumours. 'We came here to cut wood, that's what we know and that's what we would do,' they said. But a few grew curious.

They wandered off the main path. They noticed certain trees smelt sweeter. The soil beneath their feet looked different. They bent down, touched the earth and slowly began to discover things: fragrant bark, rare fruits, even gemstones lying just beneath the surface.

These few stumbled upon something extraordinary. Hidden beneath the oldest tree, covered in moss and roots, they found the philosopher's stone that could turn anything into gold.

CONSCIOUSNESS KEY

You can spend a lifetime preparing, but without purpose, there's no spark.

Vasishtha looked at me and said, 'Ram, the forest is like the world of knowledge. Most people spend their lives working hard, gathering thoughts and surviving through routine, but only a few look deeper.

'They ask, "What am I really seeking?" They go beyond reading, beyond effort, into direct experience. Those who are sincere feel the real thing, the stone that changes everything is not found by effort alone. It's found by looking differently.'

TRY THIS IN REAL LIFE

Relatable Situation

You've been exploring various self-help and spiritual techniques like journalling, guided meditations and visualizations. You're doing everything right, but it still feels like something's missing. You're hoping for a deeper shift, something that actually changes how you feel inside.

What To Do

Sit comfortably and close your eyes. Follow the steps in Appendix 2 for Heartfulness meditation.

Why This Helps

This practice takes your attention from method to experience. It helps you stop collecting tools and start connecting with what's already present in you. This practice invites real connection with the source itself.

25

Lives Come and Go, the Witness Stays

King Padman and Queen Leela were so in love that they barely noticed the world around them. They rode elephants, camels and boats, danced under the moonlight, played games and delighted in each other's company.

One day, Queen Leela told herself, *'If I die first, I'll be at peace. But if he dies before me, I won't survive the grief. I must find a way to keep his presence with me forever.'* She began to worship Goddess Saraswati with devotion, seeking a boon to preserve her husband's spirit.

The goddess appeared and offered her a blessing. Leela asked for two things:

1. That her husband's soul should never leave her home.
2. That whenever she prayed, the goddess would come to her.

Time passed, and King Padman died. Overwhelmed with sorrow, Leela kept his body and cried out to the goddess, 'Where is my husband?'

Saraswati replied, 'He is beyond the physical and mental realms. He is in the spiritual world now. I grant you the power to rise above your bodily attachments and mental desires, so that you will see him.'

With the goddess's grace, Leela could see her husband again. But he was now King Viduratha, surrounded by nobles, saints and warriors in a majestic realm. Leela longed to be seated among them, and her wish was fulfilled. But she immediately felt uncomfortable as she no longer felt like it was *her* place. The bond she remembered seemed distant. So, she withdrew from that vision and returned to her palace and sat beside the lifeless body of Padman.

She prayed to the goddess again, '*Which of these worlds is real?*'

Goddess Saraswati answered with a story: 'Once, there was a Brahmin named Vasishtha, married to Arundati. The Brahmin desired to be a mighty king. That desire led him to be reborn as King Padman. You, Leela, and your husband are the rebirths of that couple.'

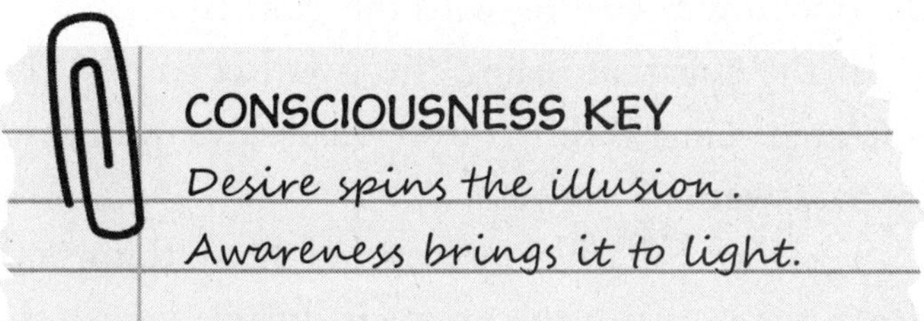

Leela was puzzled. 'But that Brahmin you showed me just now drew his last breath, and yet Padman has been ruling our kingdom for years! How can both be true?'

Saraswati smiled. 'Reality is beyond time and space. What you see as years or moments are all appearances within consciousness. A single moment in trance may feel like an age, and an age may vanish like a moment. This life is a memory in the soul. Liberation comes when one rises beyond all desires, likes and dislikes.'

The goddess took Leela on an astral journey to the Brahmin's humble house. She blessed the Brahmin's young son. Along the way, Leela remembered even more past lives as a woman, a man, a fish, a cow, a bee, a bird.

King Viduratha, too, remembered being King Padman. And astonishingly, he had another queen in that life, also named Leela, who looked just like the one now travelling with the goddess.

In the spiritual realm, the two Leelas and the liberated King Padman lived in harmony, blessed by Saraswati.

Sage Vasishtha, having narrated this to Ram, said, 'Ram, when you wake up, your dreams vanish. In the same way, this waking dream, your whole life, vanishes at death. You ask whether Leela's three husbands – the Brahmin, King Padman and King Viduratha – lived for the same length of time. The answer depends on consciousness. To one in pain, a night feels endless but to someone celebrating, it's gone in a flash. Time is only real to the mind.'

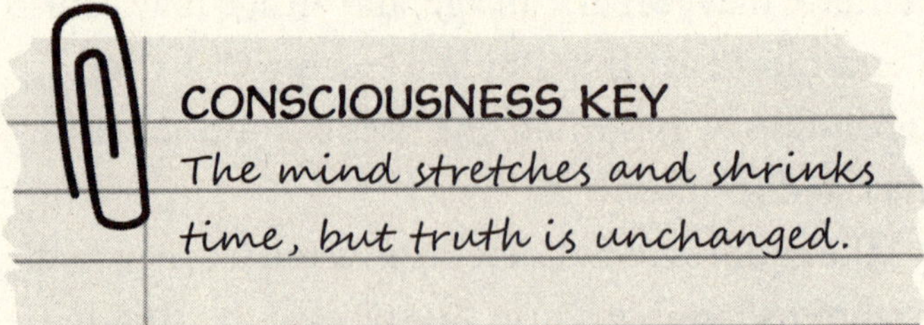

TRY THIS IN REAL LIFE

Relatable Situation

You find yourself living through unexpected changes in relationships, roles, places, beliefs. Each phase feels like a different lifetime. A part of you resists, wanting to hold on, but life keeps happening fast. It's exhausting to keep adjusting. You're searching for peace amidst all this impermanence.

What To Do

Sit quietly and go over Appendix 12, which is all about creating cheerful acceptance.

Why This Helps

When you begin to accept life as it comes, with a deep inner yes, you settle down. You stop being attached to each role, phase or outcome. In that cheerful acceptance, you glimpse what Leela discovered: The Self isn't caught in any particular moment or life. The Self is permanent.

26

Wisdom Means Not Falling Again

One lesson Laxman and I remembered during the dangerous fourteen years spent in the forest is this: Never repeat the same mistake twice. Awareness is the most important aspect of consciousness. To illustrate this, I will tell you the story of the elephant that I heard from sage Vasishtha.

In the Vindhya mountains, there once lived a mighty elephant that was strong, proud and free. One day, a hunter came into the forest carrying an iron trap. The elephant watched him set it up with its sharp edges and felt a whisper of caution. But driven by carelessness or curiosity, it stepped right into the trap.

The pain it felt was sharp and brutal as the iron dug into its legs. But the elephant, with its great inner strength and will, pulled with all its might and broke free. Bloodied but determined, it walked away into the forest, back towards freedom.

The hunter, watching from a distance, panicked. '*The elephant must be furious with me,*' he thought. '*If it finds me, it will surely take revenge.*' Afraid, he ran but didn't get far. Desperate, he climbed a nearby tree and perched on a high branch.

But the branch was slippery. In a moment of bad luck, he fell, landing right in front of the very elephant he had tried to trap.

The elephant looked at him and recognized his face. It knew the pain this man had caused. It could have crushed him in an instant. But compassion welled up inside, and it turned away and walked on, sparing the hunter's life.

CONSCIOUSNESS KEY

Real strength means to walk away without causing harm, even when you have the power to.

But the hunter did not learn; he returned with a group of men. This time, he dug a deep pit, covering it with leaves and branches to hide the danger. Days passed.

The healed elephant wandered back through the forest and reached the same clearing. It felt the earth shift beneath its weight, but it ignored that and kept walking. The ground collapsed, and it plunged into the pit.

CONSCIOUSNESS KEY

Escaping a trap is not enough. Wisdom is in not stepping into it again.

TRY THIS IN REAL LIFE

Relatable Situation

You made the same mistake again. You knew better, but acted out of habit, pressure or reaction. Now you feel the brunt of it and you want to change for good.

What To Do

Before going to bed, sit down and close your eyes. Follow the Heartfulness prayer as described in Appendix 4. After repeating it twice, sit in silence and allow yourself to absorb the feeling it creates.

Why This Helps

True change is not merely avoiding or eliminating an old habit, but it is more about remembering what matters before the moment comes again. This prayer helps you reconnect with your inner compass and prepare from the heart.

27

When Identity Becomes the Obstacle

One day I asked Sage Vasishtha, 'Everyone speaks of the importance of knowing who we are. But why is it that the more I hold on to an idea of "myself," the more troubled I feel? Can this sense of identity itself stand in the way?'

Vasishtha replied, 'Ram, identity has its use in the world, but when it hardens into ego, it becomes an obstacle. To show you how even the strongest can fall when the thought of "I" arises, let me tell you an ancient tale.'

Long ago, a great war raged between the gods and demons. Among the demons was a brilliant sorcerer-king named Sambara whose powers were immense and whose magic was unmatched. But while he was asleep, the gods struck his armies and crushed them.

When he woke up, Sambara decided to outwit the gods. So he created something that had never been created before. He made three warrior-demons who had no previous birth. They were called Dama, Vyala and Kata, later known as Bhima, Bhasa and Dridha, respectively. They were not born of any womb and had no karma, no desires, no memories. And most importantly, they had no ego. They were like elemental forces and worked like flawless machines, without hesitation, fear or doubt. In battle, they were unstoppable.

The gods panicked. Their weapons were no match against the three warrior-demons and their armies fell. The gods went to the Creator and begged for a solution. The Creator said, 'You cannot defeat them by force as they are pure will, with no self. But in their moment of victory, plant in them the seeds of ego. Give them ambition and make them restless with greed. Invite laziness, indulgence and the desire to be worshipped. Once they think of themselves as "I", they will dig their own graves.'

So the gods waited. As the demons celebrated their dominance, temptations like power, pleasure and pride were shown to them. The once-pure warriors started boasting. They began to hunger for glory and became impatient. And with that, they weakened. In the next battle, the gods easily won over them.

When King Sambara demanded they return to face punishment, the three escaped and hid in the lowest world, far from the reach of both gods and demons. There, they lived in secret and even had families.

But one day, Yama, the god of death, visited their realm. When they ignored him, Yama was offended and burnt them to death. A long and painful journey began for the three. Dama, Vyala and Kata were reborn again and again, as birds, insects, serpents, pigs and fish. From life to life, they retained their impressions. In one life, Dama was a gnat, Kata a parrot and Vyala a sparrow, living unnoticed in a royal palace.

One day, the king's minister spoke aloud of an ancient war between gods and demons. The three birds, hearing this, were struck with memories. Their eyes opened and the long sleep of ignorance ended. In that moment, the last residue of desire and ego left them.

They became calm, free and enlightened.

I listened deeply, 'Now I see, Gurudev. Those warriors were invincible until they began to think of themselves as "I." It was not their strength that failed, but their pride that weakened them.'

Vasishtha replied, 'Yes, Ram. Action without ego is pure and free. The moment "I" enters, desire, fear and doubt follow. Remember this: freedom comes not by building an identity, but by seeing beyond it.'

CONSCIOUSNESS KEY

Even the darkest journey ends when the soul awakens to its story.

TRY THIS IN REAL LIFE

Relatable Situation

You've become known as the one who always delivers, in school or at home. At first, this gave you confidence, but over time it turned into your identity. Now pausing feels like failing, and what once gave you energy has become pressure you can't step away from.

What To Do

Think of a recent moment when you felt pressure to prove yourself, to succeed, to stay in control or to meet expectations. Say inwardly, *'Even if I didn't get it all right, I'm still okay.'* Then begin Heartfulness cleaning as given in Appendix 3. Later, as you go through your day, try to remain in the state of Constant Remembrance as given in Appendix 13. Before starting any task or conversation, pause briefly. Bring your attention to your heart and feel that your actions are being guided from within your heart.

Why This Helps

The three warriors were unbeatable until pride turned their strength into weakness. In the same way, when achievement becomes identity, it exhausts us. These practices help remove that pressure and bring you back to the Self that acts freely, without the burden of 'I.'

28

The Ego Is the Last Illusion

Sage Vasishtha once told me, 'If you want to know what true peace feels like, what undisturbed rest of the soul is, you must follow the way of Uddalaka.'

Uddalaka was a famous sage, a great yogi and philosopher, who is mentioned in many Upanishads. He was the father of sage Shwetaketu and maternal grandfather of the famous Ashtavakra of the famed Ashtavakra Gita.

Let us get back to his pursuit of inner peace in his youth.

Uddalaka was curious and troubled by questions that most people bury under distractions. But he turned inwards and asked: 'How can I go beyond birth and death? How do I break the cycle of craving and regret? When will I reach the place that lies beyond the distractions of my own mind?'

To seek that place, he walked away from the world and entered a silent cave, spread deerskin over a bed of leaves and began a simple practice of meditation and self-inquiry.

He observed the world with honesty. *Moths rush into flame and burn for the sake of light. Fish get caught by their craving for taste. Elephants are trapped because they chase touch. Humans, blinded by all five senses, are trapped deeper than any of them.*

So he regulated his senses and watched his breath. He allowed thought to slow down until it was no longer the master. Even when celestial beings invited him to heaven, Uddalaka respectfully declined. 'What I seek is not a reward,' he whispered, 'but freedom from it all.'

CONSCIOUSNESS KEY

Even in the best place, you won't feel peace if your mind is restless. Peace begins when the wanting stops.

He practised breath awareness and detachment until ego itself grew distant. He whispered into the cave, 'Who invented this word "I"? What is it, really?'

He saw that 'I' is not an organ, not a muscle, not even a solid thought. It is imagination that grows wild in the mind, claiming everything.

'I sense a field of awareness inside me,' Uddalaka said, 'as wide as space and as small as an atom, not reachable by ego, thought, or desire.'

Even the gods observed him with awe and he transcended life's restlessness.

TRY THIS IN REAL LIFE

Relatable Situation

You're constantly defending your opinions in arguments or debates and feel depleted afterwards.

What To Do

Take paper and pencil outside. Sketch anything – a plant, a bench, a tree. This is called nature sketching. You don't have to be perfect in your artwork; you just have to capture your observation.

You can also try the Speech Regulation Technique from Appendix 5. If you find yourself constantly trying to assert your views or react sharply in conversations, this silent practice will be helpful.

Why This Helps

The nature sketching practice lets the ego take some rest and sharpens conscious and serene attention. Speech is where ego often shows up. Regulating how you speak calms the ego's urge to control, explain or defend. It's a subtle but powerful way to remove the 'I' and return to awareness.

29

The Soul Is Buried Under What Is Imagined

Vasishtha once said to me, 'Ram, even a little learning can transform a person with a sincere, open heart. But even oceans of scripture cannot change someone who is stiff with ego and shut down inside.'

Then he told me about a rare kind of student, a Vidyadhara, a celestial being, who once came to Kaka Bhushunda, the ancient crow-sage, for guidance.

This Vidyadhara had lived for ages. Through austerity and self-restraint, he gained a long life and mystical powers. But after lifetimes of pleasure and ego, he began to feel disgusted with himself.

He came to Bhushunda and said, 'My senses, my eyes, ears, tongue and skin, still chase external pleasure. Even after all this time, I feel pulled into desires that I thought I had outgrown. I want a teacher who can help me.'

Bhushunda looked at him with kindness and said, 'Your request comes from the right place. Think of ego as a seed,' he said. 'From that seed grows the whole tree. The roots are your senses, the soil is your ignorance and the branches are your desires. People sit like birds on this tree, thinking it's their home. But if you burn the seed, no tree grows, no birds gather and the whole show ends.'

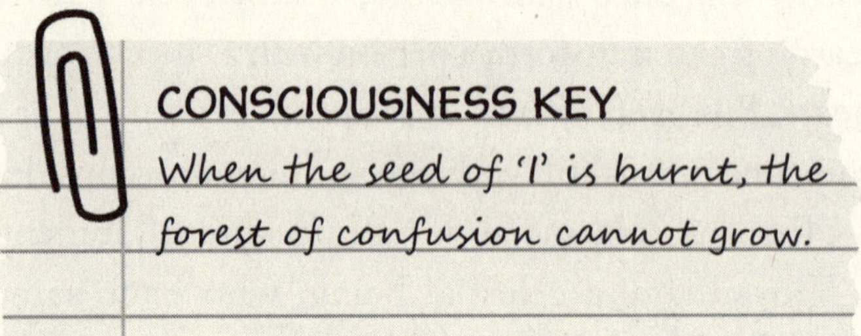

He told the Vidyadhara to burn that seed with reason, reflection, effort and faith.

'Don't be fooled again,' Bhushunda said. 'The mind, senses and ego – they all rise from not knowing who you are. That ignorance can be destroyed with the help of teachers, of sacred books, and of your own honest inner work.'

Then Bhushunda told him a story I didn't expect. 'Even Indra, the king of the gods, once forgot himself. He studied too much, thought too much and lost his strength, which allowed the demons to defeat him. He then ran away and hid inside the smallest space – an atom.

'Inside that atom, he used his imagination to create a palace. Then he created a city, and then a kingdom of gods. He had a son who ruled after him and that son had a son. Thus, a thousand generations passed. Eventually, one of those imaginary Indras became enlightened and conquered the demons again.

'And that imaginary kingdom? It still goes on.'

After a pause, Bhushunda spoke again to the Vidyadhara, 'Do you understand? Even Indra built a whole world from the seed of ego and the water of desire. So what do *you* want to plant?'

CONSCIOUSNESS KEY

If you stop imagining, the mind becomes light and the soul becomes free.

The Vidyadhara listened. He entered a trance and never came out the same. His ego dissolved, his mind became still and he found peace.

TRY THIS IN REAL LIFE

Relatable Situation

Your mind feels constantly full of imagination and daydreams and overthinks. You struggle to feel clear or rested. You know your creativity is a gift, but sometimes it leaves you foggy and scattered.

What To Do

Lie down or sit with your back supported. Close your eyes and do the relaxation technique as shared in Appendix 1. Allow the earth to heal you through its soothing energy. When each muscle relaxes, you feel completely grounded by nature.

Why This Helps

Imagination can drain you if it never pauses. This practice grounds you in the present and lets your nervous system return to normalcy and clarity.

30

What You Call God Is Still a Reflection

Once, a question arose in me and left me stunned. If everything arises from God, I wondered, then why does that first wave begin? What stirs the stillness into becoming?

'Ram,' Vasishtha said, 'this isn't the first time you've asked about the beginning of creation. In a previous life, you were my student too. And then, as now, you asked: "*Can God have an ego?*"'

He continued, 'In that earlier life, you asked, "If God is beyond qualities, beyond form and thought, how can such an entity create a world that seems full of division, names, egos and roles?"

'You asked, "Is God subject to His own illusion?"'

'And that Vasishtha had replied, "No. God doesn't have ego in the way we think. But at the edge of creation, a reflection emerges. That reflection carries a subtle feeling of identity, like the faint taste of 'I am'. That is what you call God's ego. It is the first light that arises when stillness chooses to become an experience."

He said, "It is from this light that space, time and direction get created."

But remember, Ram – that "I" is still an illusion, a sacred one, but still not the supreme. God, the Supreme Self, remains beyond even that, beyond being and non-being.'

I asked, 'Then why do so many scriptures say that God created the world consciously?'

He smiled. 'Because even the scriptures are reflections. They meet the seeker at his level of consciousness evolution. A child cannot understand formlessness, so we begin with names. A devotee cannot pray to vastness, so we speak of forms. But as you go deeper, you let even that go.

'Even light, Ram, is just a veil. Reality is what remains when light dissolves.'

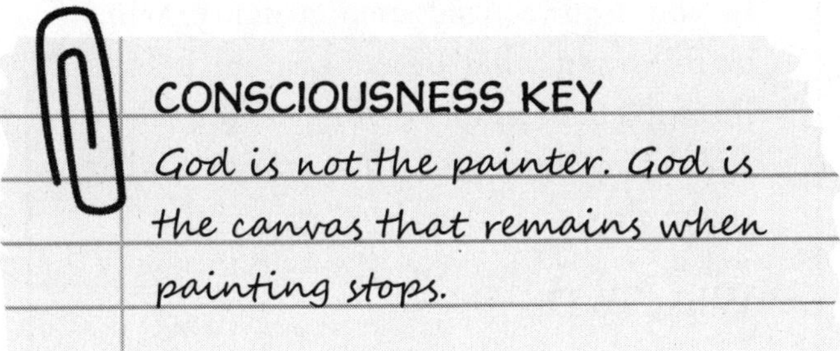

And then Vasishtha said the words that closed the loop: 'So, can God have ego? Not really. But if you must ask the question, the answer will always be a reflection, never the real. Reality can only be experienced.'

TRY THIS IN REAL LIFE

Relatable Situation

You hear people talk about God, energy or spirituality, but none of it feels real to you. You've tried meditating, praying or following what others say, but it feels incomplete or empty or forced. You're left wondering if the problem is you, or if what you're chasing isn't real to begin with.

What To Do

Offer the Heartfulness prayer as given in Appendix 4. This is not a prayer in the traditional sense. Just introspect on the meaning of the words with sincerity. Then go to bed or meditate for a few minutes.

Why This Helps

When you let go of fixed ideas about God or spirituality, your mind stops trying to control the experience. The prayer becomes a simple act of approaching the unknown without expectation.

31

The World Becomes What You Believe

Vasishtha once told me a story that felt like falling through mirrors, each one reflecting another, until I couldn't tell what was real anymore.

He said that the fourth soul-fragment of King Vipaschit, named Bhasa, once saw a giant corpse fall from the sky. The corpse was so massive, it covered the earth like a collapsed mountain. Even the very gods panicked and trembled. Only Agni, the god of fire, remained calm.

'Don't be afraid,' he told Bhasa. And then, he carried him upwards.

The world prayed to the Universal Mother who arrived with other fierce goddesses. They tore the giant body apart, and out of what remained, a new world began to emerge.

Later, Bhasa asked Agni, 'What was that corpse? Why did it fall?'

Agni told him a story.

'Once, a mighty Asura destroyed the hut of a sage. The sage cursed him to be born as a tiny gnat.

'The gnat died under the foot of a deer and became a deer. The deer died looking at a hunter and became the hunter. The hunter met a sage, who told him: "Put down your arrow and don't kill the deer. Learn to care for all sentient beings instead."

'The hunter learnt to meditate. The sage entered his heart and lit the lamp of knowledge. One day, the hunter experienced cosmic dissolution; the sage, too, experienced it because their consciousness had merged.

"How do you know if dreams are real?" the hunter asked.

The sage replied, "What you believe becomes your truth and your fate follows your belief."'

'The sage later realized that he too had been dreaming. He saw another sage enter his house and speak of calamities: wars, famine, fire. The guest said, "Sometimes, many souls are bound together

CONSCIOUSNESS KEY

Reality is what your consciousness claims as true.

by group karma. They desire alike. They act alike. They suffer alike."

And then, he predicted, "A hunter will come. He will ask questions. He will earn a boon. He will grow into a giant being, and when he no longer wants that body, it will fall as a carcass to the earth. But don't worry. New creation will rise from it."'

'Indra had once told Bhasa, "You will live many more lives, including as a deer in Ram's garden, before you are free.' And so it happened.

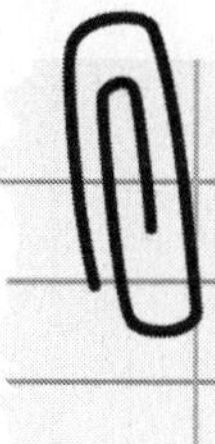

CONSCIOUSNESS KEY

Consciousness is not one thing inside a person, it is the field in which all stories appear, dissolve and begin again.

TRY THIS IN REAL LIFE

Relatable Situation

You're comparing your life with others' social media updates online. You start believing your life isn't enough.

What To Do

Do a digital cleanse ritual. Delete or mute three accounts that make you feel anxious or inferior. Replace with something neutral (nature videos, poetry or silence). After this, use the Guided Inquiry Technique from Appendix 7 and ask yourself questions like, 'What do I believe about success, beauty or worth?', 'Where did these beliefs come from?', 'Are they helping or hurting me?', 'What would I rather believe instead?', and so on.

Why This Helps

Social media comparison comes from unconscious beliefs about what a 'good life' looks like. The hunter in the story became free only when he saw through those illusions and stopped pursuing what others valued. This practice helps you do the same. When you see a belief clearly, its power dissolves and from that space, a new way of living can emerge.

32

The Soul was Never Bound by the World

One morning, I asked Sage Vasishtha a question, 'Is liberation only for those who give everything up?'

He didn't give me an explanation. He answered with a story, as usual.

Vasishtha told me about a seeker named Sutikshna who had once asked his guru, Sage Agastya, the same thing: 'Should I pursue liberation through knowledge, or through action?'

Rather than reply directly, Agastya shared a story about a young man named Karunya. He had returned home after his studies but couldn't bring himself to act. He brooded for days in thought.

Karunya's father, Sage Agnivesya, noticed this and asked, 'Why do you sit here doing nothing?'

Karunya replied, 'I am thinking of liberation. I believe the only way to attain liberation is through renunciation.'

Agnivesya shook his head. 'Before you decide that, let me tell you the story of King Arishtanemi. His journey may change the way you see things.'

And so, the story continued.

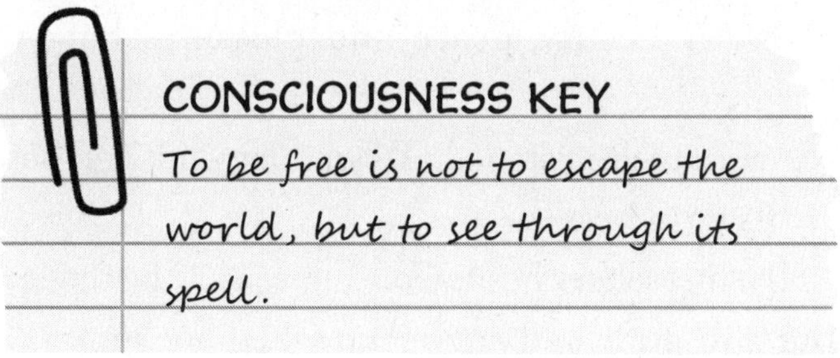

Far away, high in the Himalayan peaks, a celestial dancer named Suruchi sat in meditation, surrounded by the whispering winds and the graceful dance of peacocks.

As she sat in stillness, a divine messenger passed by. She stopped him.

'Where are you headed?' she asked.

The messenger paused and smiled. 'Let me tell you an extraordinary tale.'

And that's how we now enter the extraordinary story of King Arishtanemi.

Arishtanemi had ruled justly, fulfilled his responsibilities and then withdrew to the mountains to meditate. His devotion caught the attention of Indra, the king of the heavens, who sent a messenger to invite him to the celestial realms.

'Come to heaven, O King,' said the messenger. 'There is beauty, peace and pleasures beyond imagination.'

Arishtanemi listened. 'Tell me,' he said, 'are there any flaws in heaven?'

The messenger hesitated. 'There is joy,' he replied. 'But also pride and envy. And when one's merit is spent, the soul returns to the mortal world.'

'Why would I exchange one temporary illusion for another?' he said. 'I seek true liberation, not a fleeting paradise.'

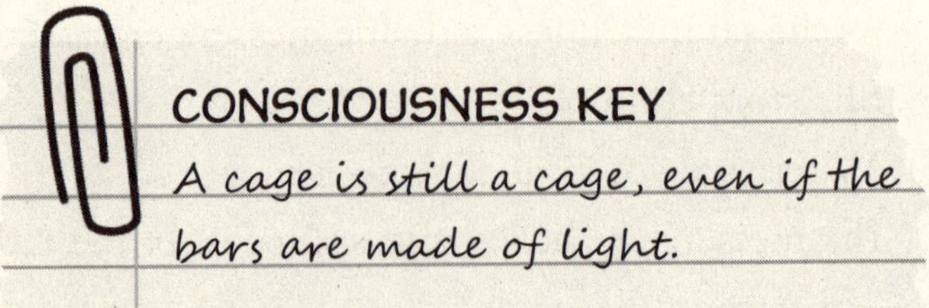

When the messenger relayed this to Indra, he was astonished. Here was someone who seeks something beyond even paradise.

Recognizing Arishtanemi's wisdom, Indra sent him to Sage Valmiki, the great teacher, for guidance, who revealed a hidden truth.

'The world is a grand illusion, like the sky appearing blue, though, in reality, it has no colour at all. What you perceive is not what truly is. The greatest illusion isn't the world around you but the belief that you are bound by it.'

Valmiki then shared what he called the Four Steps to Freedom:

Step 1: Let Go of Desires

Desires grow faster than they can be fulfilled. They unsettle the mind and stretch it thin.

Step 2: Cut the Invisible Ropes

Status, identity, memory, fear – none of these are visible but all of them can bind us. The moment you cut them off, your soul is free.

Step 3: Empty the Mind's Burden

The past, like regrets, fears and sorrows, lives in us

like the weight in a satchel. Freedom isn't about more divine knowledge. It's about setting things down from the satchel.

Step 4: Rest in Awareness

When the mind is clear and desires are gone, liberation reveals itself. It was just hidden behind layers of illusion. As these layers dissolve, we have access to the highest wisdom and feel peace.

Arishtanemi found his answers. He had no need for heaven, no fear of the world and no burdens to carry. He had found true freedom. I had always imagined freedom as something distant, waiting at the end of a long path. But the story revealed something else. The desire for freedom can turn into its own attachment.

Vasishtha had once told me that freedom isn't something we acquire. Freedom begins when we stop looking outside for what the heart already holds.

TRY THIS IN REAL LIFE

Relatable Situation

You feel trapped by the pressure to be someone – the top student, the responsible child, the one who never fails, the one who fits in. Maybe you've followed the script. Maybe you've rebelled against it. Either way, it still defines you. You start to wonder if there's anything in you that's truly free.

What To Do

As given in Appendix 15, begin meditating with a certified Heartfulness trainer. Through the Heartfulness app or a local HeartSpot, request a guided session. You don't need to prepare anything or 'get it right'. Just show up. The trainer will help you experience a deeper inner state where labels, pressures and identities begin to fade. Make this a weekly habit and notice the changes in you.

Why This Helps

The story reminds us that even the pull towards heaven can be another illusion. Real freedom is about experiencing something deeper *within* yourself. When you meditate with yogic transmission, you experience the centre that is silent and vast. The more often you return to that space, the less the outside world binds you. You realize what Arishtanemi realized – the soul was never really trapped.

33

Stop Running, You're Already Home

Sage Vasishtha and I were walking through the palace gardens one early evening. I'd been thinking for a while and finally asked, 'Gurudev, why do people suffer so much, even when no one's hurting them? Why do we make our own lives harder than they need to be?'

He answered, 'Because when the mind forgets the light of the heart, it becomes a weapon that turns inwards.'

Then he told me a story.

A long time ago, though maybe it wasn't time as we know it, the master of creation (some say it was Brahma, some say it was the Self) wandered through a forest. It was not a real forest but a symbolic one.

It was dry, wild, tangled and like a desert of the soul.

There, he saw a man whose body was covered with a thousand eyes and a thousand arms, each arm holding a different weapon, swords, spears, whips and chains.

But strangely, he was beating himself up. He was slashing, hurting and screaming. He was running in circles through thorns, through sandstorms, through pits of fire and darkness. Sometimes, he would fall into a dark hole and cry there, alone and afraid. Eventually, he'd crawl out, only to return to hurting himself again.

Then, unexpectedly, he stumbled into a lush banana grove. The shade cooled him. The wind felt gentle and cool, and he smiled, barely for a moment. But soon, he turned again and ran straight back into the forest, back into the thorns and back into the darkness.

Over and over and over again.

The Creator watched in silence. Until finally, he stepped forward and asked, 'Why are you doing this? Why are you hurting yourself, falling into pits, running through pain?'

But the man didn't stop, he didn't even pause.

He screamed, 'I am not doing anything! You're my enemy! You're the one who causes me pain!'

And then he ran away.

The Creator kept walking and found others just like him. Thousands. All hurting themselves with their own hands. Some were crying, others were running and still others were falling. Some of them were blaming others for their suffering.

But among them were a few who paused, just long enough to hear the voice.

The Creator gently asked again, 'Why do you do this?'

And they looked up. And for the first time, they *noticed* what they were doing. They stopped and turned inwards. And in the silence, a light flickered inside their hearts and they changed.

CONSCIOUSNESS KEY

You're not being punished by life. You're the one being hard on yourself and you can stop.

When Vasishtha finished the story, I just sat there speechless, as I saw myself in that man. All the time we choose pain and blame and repeat without even realizing it.

'So,' I asked, 'what did it all mean?'

Vasishtha explained, 'That man is the mind, Ram. The thousand eyes are the countless tendencies it holds and the thousand arms are its actions, flailing in every direction. The forest is this world and the thorns are attachments, cravings and fears. The dark pits are the states of despair and the banana grove is temporary, shallow peace that doesn't last. The weapons are our own thoughts and that is how we beat ourselves with guilt, comparison, regret and pride. But the moment the mind hears the voice of the teacher, the light of the heart, something changes.'

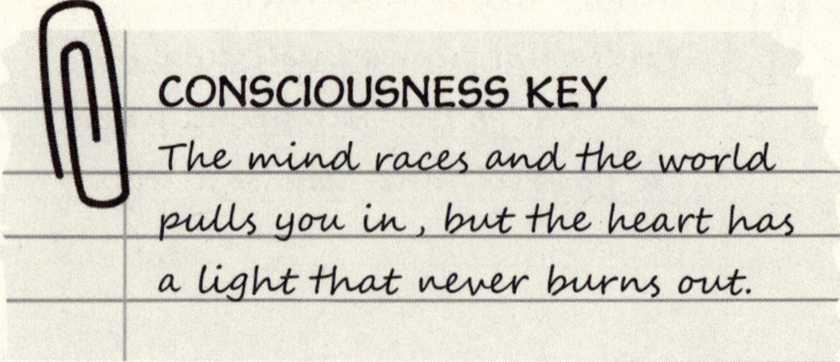

I saw how often I'd run into the same thorns. How many people are doing the same, fighting quiet battles that no one else sees? Most of us never pause long enough to hear that small voice inside say, 'It's okay, you can stop, you're safe now.'

Vasishtha placed a hand on my shoulder. 'Ram, don't be afraid of the forest, but don't forget the lamp inside you either. Most of humanity suffers because they never learnt to befriend their own mind.'

Only when the heart leads can the mind learn to heal.

TRY THIS IN REAL LIFE

Relatable Situation

You've been distracting yourself to avoid facing what's inside, scrolling, staying busy or always keeping noise around you. It works for a while, but eventually it wears you down. Nothing feels settled, because you're never still long enough to let anything land.

What To Do

Have a Heartfulness meditation session with a certified trainer. As given in Appendix 15, download the Heartfulness app and book a meditation session with a certified trainer, or connect with a trainer in person if available. Follow the trainer's guidance as they conduct a meditation focused on the heart in the presence of yogic transmission.

Why This Helps

Stillness is difficult to achieve when the mind is chaotic. A meditation session with a Trainer creates the inner condition to establish a connection. It gives you a direct experience of home inside yourself.

34

Becoming One with the Spiritual State

Vasishtha once told me the story of King Ikshvaku, who ruled long before I was born. He was the founder of my dynasty; his blood runs through my veins. One day, he stood on his palace balcony, watching the people of his city, and asked himself, 'Why is there so much suffering in this world? There is disease, heartbreak, fear and death. Why is it like this?'

Soon after, his father, Manu, the first man on the earth, came to visit.

Ikshvaku asked him with urgency, 'Who created this world? When? How big is it really?'

Manu smiled and answered, 'The world is all in

the mind, my son. It rises and falls within the divine consciousness. Just do your duty, firmly and calmly.'

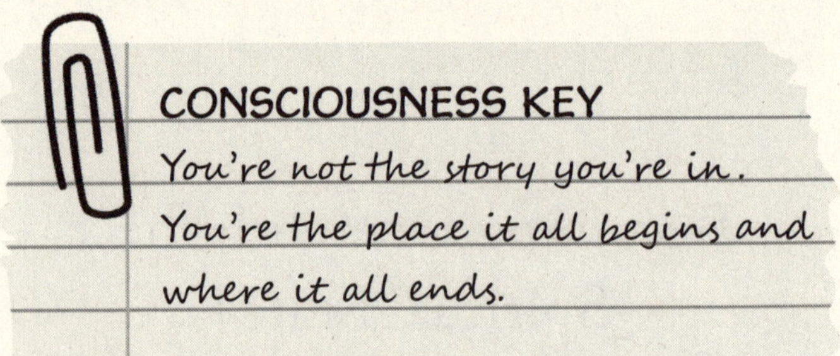

Manu continued, 'This whole world is like a painting on the screen of consciousness, that is drawn, erased and redrawn again and again.'

He told Ikshvaku that this very understanding was the greatest armour and wealth a ruler could have. Then he gave him the path:

'There are seven stages to reach this calm power:

1. First, listen to the truth.
2. Then, discuss it with a wise company.
3. Then, contemplate it.
4. Next comes meditation, when all ideas disintegrate.
5. Then you enter a stage of natural joy.
6. Then comes deep absorption, like a blissful dream.

7. Finally, you disappear into the One. The ego melts and the witness alone remains.'

He explained how the earlier stages feel like waking and dreaming, and the later ones feel like deep sleep and beyond. The final stage is Turiyatit, beyond even the fourth state of Turiya.

Manu said, 'Give up the idea that *you* are the doer. Give up thinking "*this is mine*" or "*this is hers*". Even spiritual effort, even worship, even charity cannot take you there.'

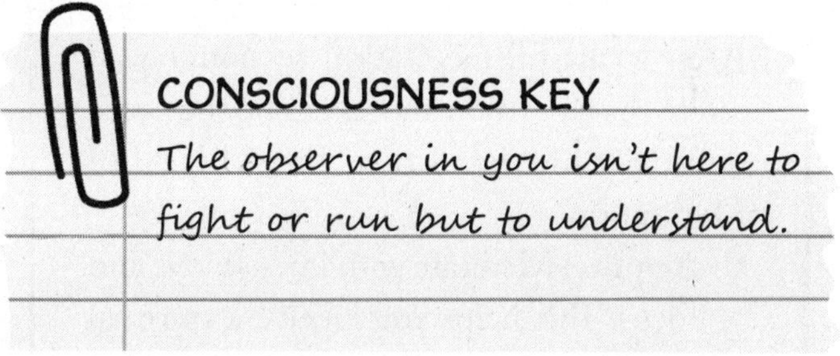

Vasishtha told me that Turiya is not something to attain. It is the natural background of the soul, where one is completely free of reaction, identity or fear. There, real life begins.

TRY THIS IN REAL LIFE

Relatable Situation

You had a meditation session that felt completely different. It was deep, quiet and beyond words. But later, life rushed back in. The stillness faded. You went back to distraction, pressure or noise. You wonder if that experience was real, and how to return to it or carry it forward.

What To Do

After a blissful meditation session, try to retain the condition and integrate the peace into daily life. I call this 'The AEIOU of Meditation'.

- **Acquire**: Meditate with intense love and focus. This helps you receive a spiritual condition.
- **Enliven**: Expand and give life to that condition with joy and gratitude and allow it to grow.
- **Imbibe**: Absorb the spiritual condition into every cell of the physical body and every part of the subtle body.

- **One with it**: Merge and become one with the condition, letting it become part of one's essence.
- **Unite**: To have union with the condition, we dissolve in the condition and allow the condition alone to exist.

AEIOU is a Heartfulness process to internalize meditative experiences, helping us to create lasting peace and accelerating spiritual evolution.

Why This Helps

This process helps retain what's received in meditation and carry it into life. Without this, even the deepest experience leaves very little impact. It trains you to hold on to the inner condition, deepen it and live from it so that peace becomes a lasting state.

Gate 4

Company of the Wise

35

Truth Doesn't Need an Audience

Once, as the discussion of the day in the court concluded, Vasishtha looked up and said, 'Some people change so quietly that you won't even notice at first. Others learn to speak like sages, but inside, the heart still wrestles with pride and doubt.'

He then added, 'Listening doesn't always mean understanding and real transformation doesn't always need an audience.'

He turned to me. 'Ram, you once met someone like that. Do you remember Sage Kundandanta?'

I nodded.

'Then tell the court whatever he shared, and also what you inferred from him.'

Thus, I narrated the tale.

Kundandanta was once the king of Malwa. He gave up his throne early and set out as a seeker.

I had met him at a gathering of sages, long ago, even before these teachings of the Yoga Vasishtha began. He was the eldest of eight brothers. All of them meditated and received divine blessings, kingdoms, wisdom and spiritual elevation, but fate had something else in store for them.

Their parents became worried that they had lost all their sons to the forest and went searching. In their panic, they stumbled into the presence of a great rishi, knocking over clay and water by accident. The rishi was angered, uttered a curse: 'Your sons will not only lose the joy of their blessings, but also have curses follow.'

That's when something unusual happened. During a meditation session, the brothers had a shared inner vision, like a powerful dream they all saw together. In it, the forces of Blessing and Curse appeared as two beings made of light and shadow. One was calm and radiant, the other was wild and sharp-edged. They were part of the brothers' own minds. The brothers realized that these forces had always been living within them, shaping their thoughts, moods and choices.

Blessing is the clarity that arises when the heart is open, whereas curse is the restlessness and confusion that takes over when the heart is clouded by ego. What they saw in that vision was a picture of what was already happening inside them. Within the vision, the two forces began to argue about which was stronger.

They brought their dispute before the father of all gods. And that father was also symbolic of the soul's own highest discernment inside the brothers' own hearts.

Curse said, 'In pure people, Blessing is rooted like a mountain. I cannot remove it.'

Blessing said, 'In selfish people, Curse is strong but short-lived.'

The purest part of the brothers' own consciousness, symbolized as the 'father of all gods' in the vision, made the ruling: 'Blessing will always lead, but Curse will trail close behind those who welcome it by being attached to ego.'

CONSCIOUSNESS KEY

Curses and blessings are not outside forces. They are mirrors of who we are when we receive them.

Eventually, the brothers left their lives of power and returned to live together in a small, humble house. One of them asked, 'How can the vastness we experienced now be contained in this small house?'

The divine being within their heart replied, 'The vastness is within you, the universe is not in the house, it is in your mind.'

Until then, Kundandanta had been what Vasishtha later called an 'upside-down ascetic'. That means someone who gives up the outside world, the throne, the title, the wealth, but still feels attached to his personal identity. Kundandanta had let go of his kingdom but not his need to be known as a wise man. He was attached to the image of being a serious and special seeker. He appeared free, but his mind was full of striving – it had goals and the pride of renunciation. He wore the identity of a seeker like a badge, shiny on the outside but gross on the inside.

One day, grieving and burdened, he came across a silent sage meditating beneath a kadamba tree. The sage opened his eyes and said, 'You are carrying too much within you. Let go of it, and peace will come on its own.' Then he paused and added, 'But you won't benefit from my words. Go to Ayodhya and spend time with Vasishtha. When you are ready, his teachings will help your consciousness to evolve.'

So Kundandanta came to Vasishtha, sat silently in his presence and just listened.

Later, Vasishtha asked him what he had understood.

Kundandanta replied, 'I've stopped asking for more knowledge. I used to think that knowing something was the same as understanding it. Now, I simply absorb what I have learnt and it becomes part of me.'

Vasishtha nodded. 'There is more truth in silent introspection than in a thousand clever questions.' Then he looked at me and simply said, 'Ram, do you understand?' And I understood.

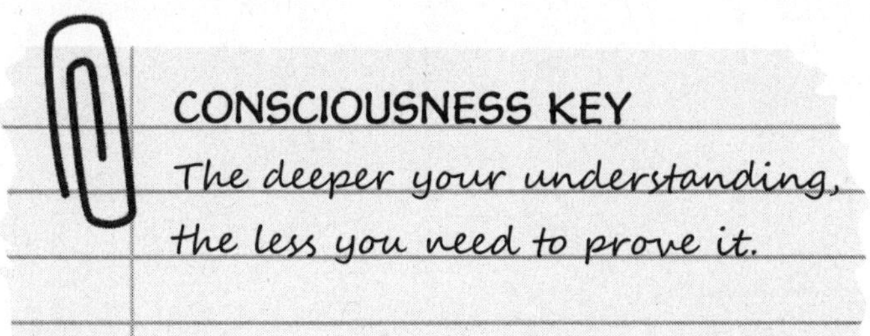

Long after the court had dispersed, I met Sage Vasishtha and asked him another question, 'What is the nature of enlightenment, then?'

Vasishtha turned the question back on me. 'If the world is a formless dream, how do we see and feel it?'

I answered, 'There was no world that was created. Just as water reflects light but is not the light, the soul reflects illusion, but when it turns away from the reflection, it finds peace.'

'And what do you feel?' he asked.

'I feel present.'

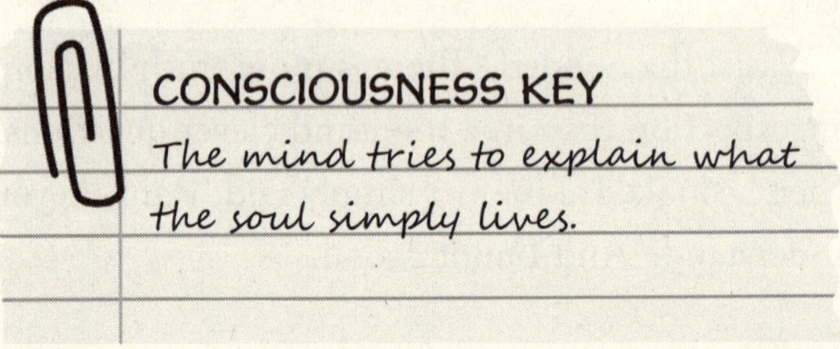

TRY THIS IN REAL LIFE

Relatable Situation

You've started to grow internally, maybe you're reflecting more, meditating or becoming calmer. But no one seems to notice. You're tempted to prove it, to show that you've changed. A part of you still wants validation before you fully trust yourself.

What To Do

Gently bring your attention to your heart. As explained in Appendix 13, practice Constant Remembrance and connect yourself to the deepest core of your heart before beginning any activity. Return to this remembrance throughout the day whenever you pause.

Why This Helps

Inner change doesn't need an audience. This practice helps you stay connected to your deeper self that doesn't need to be validated.

36

Stillness Within Action

Some meetings are planned, and some meetings feel like they have finished long before they happen.

Vasishtha once said, 'Some friendships begin in the palace but reach their truth only in the forest.' Then he told me about King Parigha and King Suraghu.

King Parigha ruled Persia during a devastating famine. His people died by the thousands as crops failed and children starved.

Parigha tried everything from prayers to policies and aid, but nothing worked. The pain of watching his kingdom collapse under nature's indifference became unbearable.

One night, he left his palace and walked deep into a forest. He ate dry leaves and, in time, became known as Parnada, the Leaf-Eater Sage. Through years of austerity, solitude and silence, he processed his grief. His mind quieted enough for him to experience stillness and, eventually, he wandered again to meet life as it came.

One day, he arrived at the city of Hemaja, where he met an old friend: King Suraghu of the Kiratas. They had once spoken of strategy and empire. But now they spoke of something else.

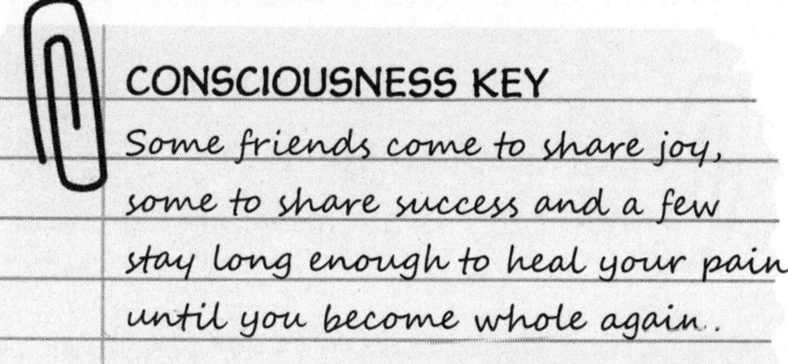

Parnada asked Suraghu, 'Have you reached the kind of rest that does not return to restlessness and where you feel neither hope nor fear?

Suraghu smiled. 'Yes,' he said, 'but I did not leave this world. I continued to do my duties and I made difficult decisions. I experienced both pain and joy. Real peace does not come from silence alone. It comes when the mind lets go of its likes and dislikes.'

Parnada saw in Suraghu the same depth he had found in the mountains, but it was rooted in action.

Suraghu said, 'Nothing in life is truly disgusting or special. Things appear, change and pass. When you have clarity within you, you can make conscious choices. You can care for others without losing your sense of direction. You can take charge without letting pride control you.'

Parnada saw that grief can lead to detachment, and detachment can return to love, without fear.

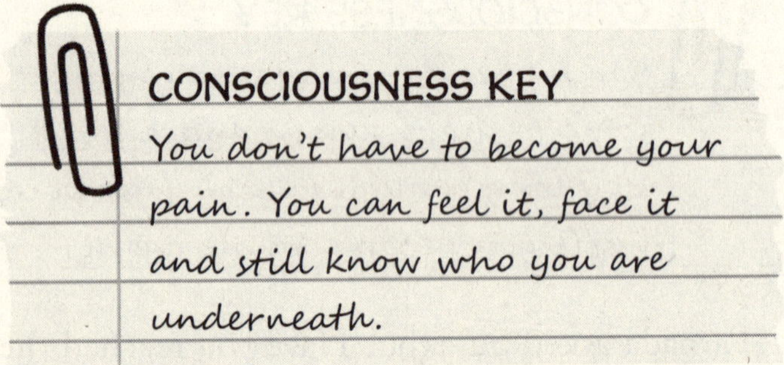

Two kings, once full of ambition, hugged now, full of knowing. Then they bowed to each other and parted ways. Their truths live forever in the space between a goodbye and a smile.

TRY THIS IN REAL LIFE

Relatable Situation

Your schedule is full. Even in your free time, there's something to do. You go from one task to another without a real break. You get things done, but there's no life or joy in you. It feels like you can only rest when everything is over.

What To Do

Take a short walk in nature for about ten to fifteen minutes. As you walk, keep a light awareness on your heart. Don't try to meditate or focus on your breath. Just walk normally while staying connected to the centre in your heart. Let the legs move, but let the mind stay anchored. You can also be in Constant Remembrance as given in Appendix 13.

Why This Helps

You don't have to stop any activity to feel at ease. This practice helps you stay focused and centred while life continues. It reflects the story's message: Calm doesn't mean stopping action but staying grounded.

37

Put the Heart Before the Mind

Vasishtha once told me, 'Ram, grief shared between friends becomes devotion. But if that grief turns inwards and festers, it becomes distraction and chaos.'

Then he told me the story of Bhasa and Vilasa, two students of Sage Atri, whose paths diverged in sorrow but united in wisdom.

In the flowering mountains near Sahya, there was a beautiful forest hermitage run by Sage Atri. It was a place of peace, learning and beauty, filled with waterfalls and the songs of birds.

Two boys, Bhasa and Vilasa, grew up in that ashram like two halves of one spirit. But then, without warning, their parents passed away. The boys were still young when they performed the funeral rites. Their hearts cried in grief and they wandered alone.

Years passed.

Both boys meditated and lived in silence in the forests in austerity. But they did not receive enlightenment. Then, one day in their old age, they met again.

CONSCIOUSNESS KEY

Distance starts when we stop understanding each other's hearts.

Vilasa looked at Bhasa and asked, 'Has your heart found peace?'

Bhasa replied, 'Not yet. How can it, when I still cling to ideas like "this is my friend" or "that is my enemy"? As long as I mistake this body for myself, peace stays far away.'

He added, 'The mind is like a wild elephant. Even if you bind it with effort and discipline, it tears free and runs towards desire. One desire meets another and they trample everything in their path, until time finally weakens the body, and it dies.'

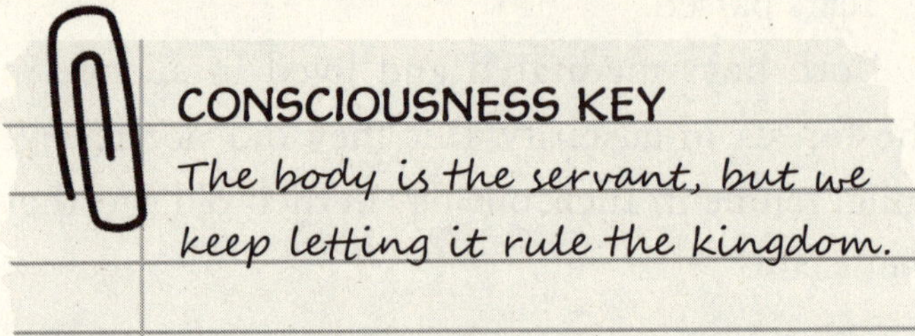

Bhasa continued, 'My mind is always busy, thinking about the past, chasing the future, doubting the present. When I try to hold it still, it slips through me like water.'

Vilasa nodded. 'Then let's stop pretending to know. Let's learn together.'

And so they did. But this time, instead of knowledge, they pursued clarity. Through meditation, humility and companionship, they received what they had both missed.

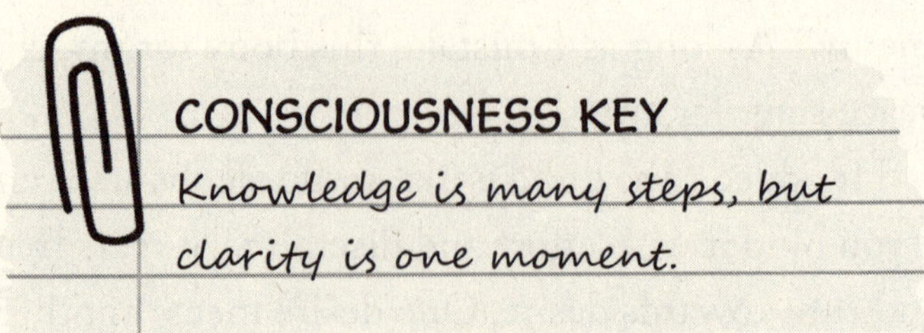

At the end of this tale, Vasishtha told me, 'Some try to control the mind through breath, or through gaze or through sound, but these are superficial techniques. You may try them and respect them, but there is a better way.'

He then explained how the feeling heart can harmonize the restless mind. He said, 'The physical heart continues its beat. But the spiritual heart contains consciousness. When the spiritual heart is purified, the mind is balanced and in harmony.'

TRY THIS IN REAL LIFE

Relatable Situation

You feel uneasy around someone. Maybe they've hurt you before or maybe there's an unspoken tension that never got resolved. Their presence brings up anxiety, mistrust or even fear, even if they're polite or distant now. You try to avoid them, but the emotional charge still lingers inside.

What To Do

Practise seeding positive thoughts as given in Appendix 10. You plant thoughts of peace and goodwill in the person in question here and clear out the inner fear, resentment or defensiveness that may still be stored within you throw them out.

Why This Helps

This practice clears the emotional residue that builds up when you keep replaying past interactions or imagining future ones. It removes the fear and resets your heart's inner relationship with that person, even if nothing changes outside. Over time, your energy towards them becomes neutral or kind, and that alone can dissolve invisible barriers.

38

The Riddles That Silenced a Ghost

Vasishtha once told me a strange story, part riddle, part revelation.

There was once a king who walked through his kingdom at night to make sure everyone was safe. His people trusted him, and he took that trust seriously.

One night, he was stopped by a Vetala, a ghost-like creature that lives on the edge of worlds, feeding on fear, pride and ignorance.

The Vetala said, 'You're tonight's meal. But I'm not unreasonable. If you can answer my questions, I will let you go.'

The king had enough power to destroy the ghost with a glance. But he also knew his dharma – to respond to every voice in his kingdom. So he agreed.

The Vetala asked, 'What is the one thing in a man that travels through dream after dream, takes on form after form, yet never abandons its original nature?'

'Which sun lights the worlds with understanding?'

'Which wind fills the stars through presence?'

'What is the hidden particle wrapped in countless sheaths, like a banana stem?'

The king closed his eyes. Then he answered, 'It is consciousness that travels through all dreams. It is the light of understanding that illuminates all things. It is the breath of presence that fills the stars. And the seed of the world or the essence of reality is covered by layers upon layers. It is the Self, the formless spark at the centre of everything.

The hunger of the Vetala vanished, and it began to meditate on the essence of that reality.

Vasishtha smiled as he told me this. 'Consciousness is the only thing that doesn't come and go. Everything else – ghosts, kings, questions, forms – they're ripples. But you are the witness.'

TRY THIS IN REAL LIFE

Relatable Situation

A past mistake or moment keeps haunting you and won't let go.

What To Do

Do left-nostril breathing technique as given in Appendix 8.

Why This Helps

Anchoring the breath soothes mental spirals and shifts our focus to the present.

39

Worship Begins Where Form Ends

One day, Vasishtha told me about a sacred meeting he had long ago that transformed the way he worshipped and understood the real purpose of spiritual life.

He had been meditating on the mountains when he suddenly opened his eyes and saw Shiva approaching, with Gauri by his side and Nandi leading the way. Vasishtha offered flowers in reverence.

Shiva asked, 'Have you found peace within? Do your desires no longer disturb your meditation? Have you crossed the fears that bind humanity?'

Vasishtha replied with humility, 'With your grace, I've been able to walk this path. But tell me,

Lord, what is the best way to worship the divine so we may be fulfilled and free?'

Shiva replied, 'Which god do you worship, Brahma, Vishnu, Lakshmi, Saraswati? And how can a finite body grasp the infinite presence of the true God? Worship done through idols and images may bring small rewards, but it is still outwards. Real worship is not outside. It is the bliss of the soul knowing its own source.'

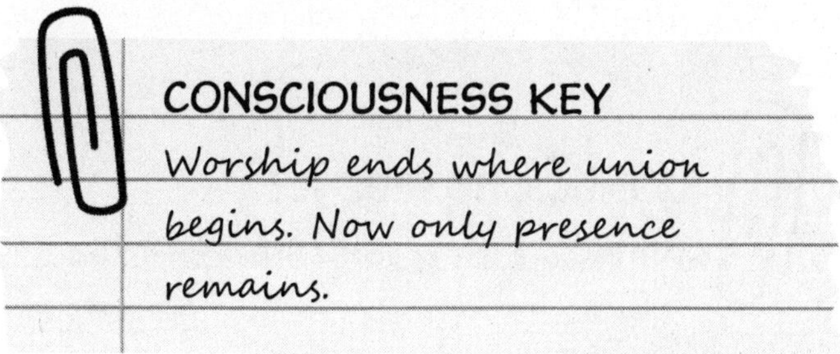

Shiva continued, 'This world, Vasishtha, is an appearance inside the sphere of consciousness. Everything you see, including your body and your wife's heart, is pervaded by that same divine consciousness. God is in the vacuum of your heart, beyond mind, beyond senses, beyond all the layers of body and personality. To meditate there, is to enter the true temple.'

Then Vasishtha asked, 'If consciousness is everywhere, why do people say someone has "died" when that consciousness leaves the body?'

Shiva replied, 'Because consciousness has forgotten itself. Like a bright light is covered in soot or masked by something else, when it forgets its purity, it believes in its smallness. Then comes ignorance, disease, death. But the Supreme Being has never gone anywhere. It is simply covered by our forgetting.'

CONSCIOUSNESS KEY

When we stop remembering the divine in the heart, we forget who we are. Real success is remembering again.

Vasishtha took Shiva's words to heart. He continued to participate in outer rituals as needed, but his true worship became inward, anchored in the living presence of the spirit within.

TRY THIS IN REAL LIFE

Relatable Situation

You've outgrown the version of god or spirituality you once followed. It could be something you were taught or something you built yourself. You're just not sure what's next. The space that opened up feels empty now.

What To Do

Offer the Heartfulness prayer as given in Appendix 4. It is just an act of offering to the unknown or a connection to the formless and nameless source beyond our knowing.

Why This Helps

When something you used to follow or believe in no longer retains the same importance or significance, there is a feeling of needing to find a quick replacement. This practice helps you stay in that in-between space so that the next spiritual anchor emerges naturally.

40

Freedom Needs No Beginning

One morning in Ayodhya, the air was crisp and the peepal leaves shimmered with dew like they were holding the memory of the night. Sage Vasishtha sat calmly on the stone bench near the lotus pond, his eyes resting on the horizon. He looked like someone who had seen the sunrise with his soul. I, on the other hand, was pacing nearby, caught between all the wisdom I'd heard and the questions it had stirred up.

'Gurudev,' I asked, 'Is there anyone who has never felt the pull of attachment? Someone who didn't have to struggle to let go because they were already free?'

He raised an eyebrow. 'Would you like to hear the story of the parrot who was already enlightened?'

Obviously, I said yes.

According to some, Shuka was born to the great Sage Vyasa. He was the compiler of the Vedas and the narrator of the Mahabharata.

This story begins with Lord Shiva about to reveal the secret of immortality to his wife, Parvati. The atmosphere was sacred. Shiva asked that no one else be present. He then told Parvati to make a humming sound as a signal that she's listening. Parvati hummed along, but halfway through, she dozed off.

Without their knowledge, a parrot chick, newly hatched, was nearby. And it listened and mimicked the humming sound.

Shiva finishes the entire teaching and turns to find Parvati resting. He realized that someone else was actually humming. And so, the divine chase began.

Shiva pursued the little parrot with divine fury. The parrot zoomed into a forest and swooped into the open mouth of Vyasa's wife, who just happened to be yawning at that moment.

Vyasa intervened and said, 'O Lord. If the parrot now knows the secret of immortality, there's no point in destroying him. It's too late. Knowledge, once given, cannot be unlearnt.'

Shiva agreed.

Vyasa turns to his wife and says, 'Dear, could you kindly deliver the parrot?'

The parrot refused to come out. He said, 'I'm not coming out. Because then I'll be your son. I want moksha, not relationships. Attachment leads to bondage and I'm not interested.'

Vyasa's wife was now pregnant with a parrot soul that refused to be born for twelve years. She endured twelve years of growing discomfort, carrying someone who was actively avoiding personhood.

Vyasa now prayed to Vishnu for help.

Vishnu, who was already on earth as Krishna, showed up and said, 'Come out. You have my word. No one will bind you. You shall be free from attachment. You will attain liberation.'

Satisfied, the parrot finally emerged in human form, glowing with clarity and was named Shuka. He was born enlightened.

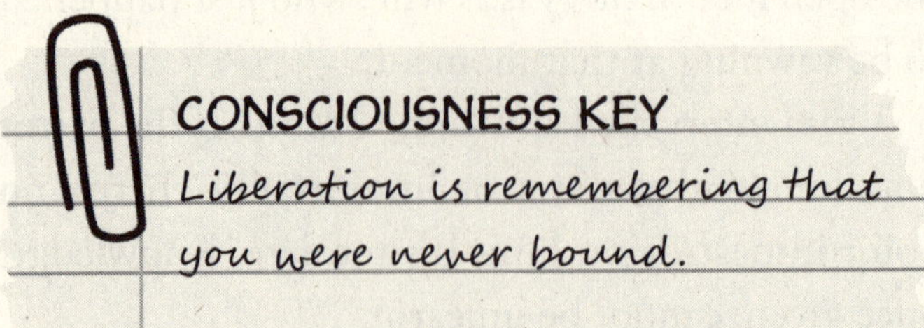

Shuka was different. While other kids were learning the alphabet, he was asking about the nature of the Self. While others played with sticks, he meditated under trees. His mind was sharp. Vyasa, despite being a great sage himself, noticed something extraordinary in his son. So he sent him to the legendary King Janaka, the philosopher-king who was known to rule like a sage and live like a renunciate.

Janaka recognized Shuka's state immediately.

He said. 'Most souls progress through the four stages of life: student, householder, forest dweller, monk. But you have already transcended the need for them.'

Shuka, however, wasn't arrogant about it. He asked questions, sought clarity and bowed with humility. Eventually, Janaka finished his teaching and said, 'You're free. Always were.'

In time, Shuka narrated a brief version of the Bhagavata Purana to King Parikshit, the grandnephew of Lord Krishna, who had only seven days to live due to a curse. After fulfilling his purpose, Shuka simply walked into a mountain cave and vanished into the stones.

Some say the cave still holds his energy. Some say he never left. Shuka came into this world without asking to be born. He was a mirror reflecting what the soul looks like without the dust.

TRY THIS IN REAL LIFE

Relatable Situation

Life is mostly fine. But even in calm moments, there's a habit of waiting for the next insight, the next breakthrough, the next version of yourself. It feels like you're always preparing for something, but not yet arriving at it.

What To Do

Sit comfortably and close your eyes. Follow the steps in Appendix 2 and try Heartfulness meditation. Bring your attention to your heart. Suppose that the source of light is already present there. Once a week have an individual meditation session with a certified Heartfulness trainer as shared in Appendix 15.

Why This Helps

Freedom doesn't begin at some future moment. It is earned through small sure steps.

41

Lead from the Soul, Not the Throne

Vasishtha once told me the story of a mountain king of the Kirata tribe, who lived near Mount Kailash. Their chief was a man named Suraghu. He was strong and brave, with skin the colour of the midday sun and hair like bright gold. His people ate fruits, roots and flowers under the shade of trees. Suraghu ruled with fairness. He punished crimes with justice. Yet restlessness lingered, a sense that justice alone was not enough to bring peace.

'Every time I pass judgment,' he told himself, 'even when it is right, someone suffers. I feel their pain. I do what I must, but my heart is heavy.'

When Sage Mandavya visited his kingdom, Suraghu shared his inner burden.

Mandavya said, 'Sit quietly and introspect. The answer is already within you.

'The great ones remember who they truly are, and that's why the chaos doesn't affect them. The soul is vast. The mind is small. Let go of the small.'

Suraghu listened. Then he sat alone under a tree.

'What belongs to me?' he asked himself. 'This city does not belong to me. Neither does this forest. This body does not belong to me, nor the mind.

What remains is this light in my heart that is eternal. This is who I am.'

CONSCIOUSNESS KEY

Power can be taken. Possessions can be lost. But the one who rules from within cannot be removed.

From that moment, Suraghu ruled the same land, gave the same judgments, offered the same care, but inwardly, he was untouched. A 100 years passed. When he finally left his body, he left without fear, longing or doubt. He had already returned home long ago, to the Self.

CONSCIOUSNESS KEY

When your actions come from the soul and not the ego, even kingship is a meditation.

TRY THIS IN REAL LIFE

Relatable Situation

You're in a position of leadership – at school, at home, in your group. Others expect you to lead, decide, manage. You want to do it well. But you feel pressure rather than purposeful.

What To Do

Each evening, sit in silence and begin Heartfulness cleaning as given in Appendix 3. Allow the pressure, subtle pride and the weight of the role to leave your system through the back and let yourself feel peace and divinity.

Why This Helps

Leadership leaves impressions on your system. This practice clears the inner load of leading, so you can return to the true purpose of leadership, which is an act of service.

Beyond the Gates

Arrival

42

The Seer Is Not What It Sees

One afternoon, after a long silence between us, Vasishtha looked at me and said, 'Ram, what we call soul, Self or even God is like a giant crystal rock that is clear and yet contains nothing. Everything that exists is seen as a reflection within it.'

I had to ask, 'Is it alive or inert?'

He smiled. 'It is neither as it is not a thing. It allows all things to appear and you can certainly see the five elements reflected in it. I have sat within it, deep in its heart, and you could too, if you wished.'

I closed my eyes and looked within: a vast, clear presence, without centre or edge. The more I tried to describe it, the more I realized it could not be named. And yet … it *was*.

CONSCIOUSNESS KEY

Even the subtlest 'I' is the beginning of illusion.

Vasishtha told me, 'The wise one sees this presence in every being, and so treats all as extensions of the Self. The ignorant one sees only bodies and misses the truth of what's reflecting in them.'

He urged me, 'Give up your doubts and go beyond even light, even truth. Reach the formless and remain in it. For the wise man, his best friend is his own good conduct. His wives are calmness, friendliness, sameness. His children are purity, simplicity and meditation.'

And then he said something very thought provoking, 'Even though people know their dreams are false, they still believe their present waking life is real.'

CONSCIOUSNESS KEY

The world is a sculpture carved into your consciousness by the chisel of thought.

TRY THIS IN REAL LIFE

Relatable Situation

You've ended a long relationship, left a role or group where your identity was deeply invested, or finished a life chapter you were emotionally tied to, and now you feel like you've lost your place in the world.

What To Do

Sit comfortably and do the ocean of peace technique as given in Appendix 6. Let the waves of peace wash over you, removing every covering that is no longer needed, like identities, roles, attachments.

Why This Helps

When identity dissolves, the system goes through a spiritual reset. This practice gives you that sacred inner bath, allowing stillness and silence to become your home again.

43

Only the Self Remains

One morning, Vasishtha said something that caught me off guard.

'Ram,' he said, 'do you know this is not the first time we've had this conversation? In a previous age, in another body, you were once my student. And you asked me a question I remember well.'

I sat up, intrigued.

He continued, 'You asked, "What remains after the great dissolution? When everything is swept away in the cosmic flood – the mountains, the sages, the stars – what is left behind?"'

Vasishtha replied, 'My answer then was the same as it is now. Everything, including angels, humans, the earth, rivers, light, time, all of it dissolves. Just as objects disappear after a dream, so too does the universe after a kalpa ends. But one thing remains and that is the great emptiness of divine consciousness, which is the source of all beginnings.'

'But Gurudev,' I had asked then, as I ask now, 'how can what is become what is not? How can something disappear completely?'

Vasishtha had replied, 'All things you see – phenomena and appearances – are delusions. They are not real; they are like the scenes of a dream. The world is a reflection in the mirror of consciousness. Whether the mirror reflects a lot or not, the mirror remains.'

'This vast emptiness, this supreme awareness, reveals and conceals all forms, but itself remains untouched.'

CONSCIOUSNESS KEY

What disappears was never truly yours. What stays was never truly 'you'. Only the seer remains.

Vasishtha told me the rest: 'The soul that gets caught up in the illusion suffers. The soul that sees it for what it is becomes free.

To the ignorant, everything appears everywhere. To the wise, nothing exists independently. Everything is only shimmering on the screen of mind.'

Then, in words that felt as though they had been waiting lifetimes to return, he said: 'Ram, rely on the pure, Supreme Self. Let its stillness be your root and let its clarity be your sky.

Delight in the soul.

Keep peace in your mind.

Rule with justice.

Do your duties.

Treat all beings with equal love.

But inwardly, know that nothing ever truly begins or ends. Only the Self remains.'

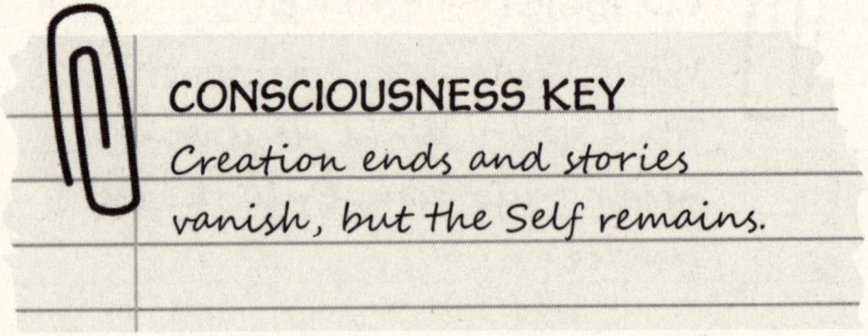

TRY THIS IN REAL LIFE

Relatable Situation

You've been living in reaction, constantly adjusting to how others see you, what the world expects or how situations unfold. Slowly, you've stopped hearing your own inner voice, which is the voice of your heart.

What To Do

Sit down and close your eyes and remember the Prayerful Suggestion #3 from Appendix 11. Suppose everyone is filled with love and all distractions and disturbances faced by the world are going away.

Why This Helps

When you have too many expectations, it becomes hard to feel who you are beneath it all. This practice helps you pause, clear out the noise and reconnect with a part of yourself that isn't defined by pressure, performance or identity.

44

Remembering What the Soul Always Knew

For twenty-two days, I had listened, questioned, wept, laughed and sat in stillness as Sage Vasishtha poured the light of truth into my heart, and now, the teaching has concluded.

What came next was something I could never have imagined.

As Vasishtha became silent, the skies seemed to respond. From the heavens descended radiant Siddhas, eternal beings of light. With them came saints, sages and angels. Even the wind paused to listen.

They bowed to Vasishtha and said, 'We have heard thousands of discourses on enlightenment since the beginning of time. But never have our minds been so moved, our hearts transformed, like they have been through this teaching.'

People of Ayodhya stood in awe. My father, King Dasaratha, was overwhelmed with gratitude. He offered Vasishtha all his wealth and kingdom to use for a great hermitage and teaching centre, but Vasishtha declined with grace.

'It is not riches that matter,' he said. 'It is an honour that you offer. And you, O King, have given that honour in abundance. Rule your kingdom wisely, that will be your offering.'

I stepped forward, my heart overflowing. I placed flowers at my Guru's feet and tears filled my eyes. I was not the same Ram who had begun this journey. My brothers, Lakshman, Bharat and Shatrughan also bowed in reverence.

Great sages like Narada, Vamadeva, Atri, Sandilya and Bharadwaja offered blessings and praise. 'You have expanded our consciousness,' they said. 'You have purified our hearts and sharpened our discipline. May your words ripple across all time.'

Then he looked at me and said, 'Ram, now describe your state.'

'My teacher,' I said, 'thanks to your guidance, I feel serene, pure and balanced. The light within is brighter than any light outside. I will perform my duties without attachment. I will live as if all this is real, and yet be rooted in what is eternal. I have no longing, no fear and no pride. I only have peace.'

Vasishtha nodded. 'Now go, serve Sage Vishwamitra and protect his sacrifices. Then serve your father and rule this land with justice. You have been purified like gold in fire. The waters of divine knowledge have washed away all impurities and your soul is awake now. Though you appear in the same body, you have become a new being.'

I could feel that I was no longer carrying old thoughts or desires. There was only clarity, peace and joy.

Lakshman said, 'I too am free of all the doubts I've carried through lifetimes.'

Shatrughan added, 'I feel light, single and whole.'

Bharat smiled, radiant and calm.

Vishwamitra rose and spoke, 'To have heard this discourse is like bathing in the Ganga a thousand times.'

Narada added, 'What we have heard today, neither men nor angels have heard before. Our ears have been sanctified.'

My father stood and declared, 'By the merit of many lifetimes, we are blessed to hear this sacred teaching.'

Vasishtha turned to him and said, 'Now, O King, honour all the sages and guests here.'

King Dasaratha ordered a grand celebration. Gifts of gold, silver, cattle and food were given freely. For seven days, the entire kingdom rejoiced.

We had remembered the light within.

CONSCIOUSNESS KEY

True celebration is not for a person; it is for the truth that wakes up inside them.

TRY THIS IN REAL LIFE

Relatable Situation

You once knew what felt right. Over time, that connection faded. You've been looking outside for answers, but the link to your inner Self is missing.

What To Do

Do the universal prayer given in Appendix 14.

Why This Helps

This isn't a prayer in the traditional sense of asking for help, but a gesture of belonging and a reminder that we're part of a shared spiritual current, connected to the larger, caring heart of humanity.

Conclusion

After the Last Question

Why I Read the Yoga Vasishtha Again and Again and How It Helped Me Find the Real Treasure Within

When the story begins, Prince Ram is a seeker filled with questions. Surrounded by wisdom and greatness, he still feels a lack of inner direction. He hasn't yet found his place in life's deeper purpose. At first, he looks outwards, trying to understand the world. But over time, his focus turns inwards, towards that which doesn't change. That's where true learning begins. He starts to see why consciousness is at the heart of it all. But he also learns that awareness alone isn't enough and that we must still act and do what is right.

Ages after Vasishtha and Ram lived, another wise man gave very similar advice to another prince. And again, it was a call for action: a life of duty, lived without attachment or repulsion. Krishna, the leader of Dwarka, counselled Arjuna that real wisdom lies in acting without worrying about results, in doing one's duty without being bound by it. He too urged a life of complete engagement, free from attachment.

At one point, Krishna says:

Yas tv ātma-ratir eva syād ātma-tṛptaś ca mānavaḥ
Ātmani eva ca santuṣṭas tasya kāryaṁ na vidyate
(Bhagavad Gita 3.17)

(But the one who delights in the Self alone, who is satisfied in the Self and content in the Self alone – for that person, there is no duty.)

He then adds:

Tasmād asaktaḥ satataṁ kāryaṁ karma samācara
Asakto hy ācaran karma param āpnoti pūruṣaḥ
(Bhagavad Gita 3.19)

(Therefore, without attachment, constantly perform your duty. For by performing actions without attachment, one attains the supreme.)

These verses may seem contradictory at first. One says, there is no duty; another says, perform all duties. But they are not contradictory. There is a secret hidden in this apparent contradiction. They point to balance: inward freedom, outward action. The wise act not because they are bound to act but because their action sustains harmony. Krishna continues in Chapter 3, Verse 20:

Karmaṇaiva hi saṁsiddhim āsthitā janakādayaḥ
Loka-saṅgraham evāpi saṁpaśyan kartum arhasi

(Janaka and others attained perfection through action alone. You too should act, having the welfare of the world in view.)

This message harmonizes beautifully with Vasishtha's teachings to Lord Ram in the Yoga Vasishtha. My take-home message is this: We have to give up all desires, attachments, sufferings, egoism, pride, shame and expectations inwardly. But outwardly, we have to act correctly, do our duties perfectly, as if it is all real.

In his early seeking, Ram pursued teachings and philosophy. Over time, he began to recognize that peace arises from inner clarity. Even this realization, this enlightenment, will not come if we remain idle or passive. We have to work for it, meditate, contemplate and remain aware. Even after realization, we must stabilize it, remember it constantly and live in its remembrance. We cannot afford to forget it.

This is how Lord Ram lived. Outside, there were struggles and suffering. But within his heart, there was balance, peace, bliss and clarity. This inner state made him the guide and shelter for everyone around him. Those who feel stirred by Ram's story may find in that very restlessness a sign that they are ready. Realization shaped the way he engaged with life, and the spiritual elevation he had acquired was reflected in the way he ruled and cared. His permanent state of realization led to the greatest of historical achievements. He defeated an evil emperor and ruled his own kingdom as an ideal king, so much so that even today, the phrase 'Ram Rajya' is used to describe perfect governance. He became a role model, and most of it can be attributed to the inner transformation he underwent as a young boy after imbibing wisdom from Vasishtha and weaponry from Vishwamitra. It is a fully human story, and miraculously effective.

We may read the Yoga Vasishtha again and again. Its depths may not reveal themselves at first. But over time, like digging into sacred ground, the real treasure within begins to shine.

Now, if you ask me why I kept returning to the Yoga Vasishtha, here is my honest answer. At first, I wasn't sure why I was reading it. Some passages felt abstract, others too logical, and some beyond logic, purely intuitive. Some were difficult to grasp, and some very simple. Some were magical and otherworldly.

Then came a moment in meditation. I realized something simple: Nothing – not the objects, not the sounds, not even the so-called real world – had meaning until I switched on my instruments of perception. If the eyes are shut, ears closed, skin numbed, tongue silent, then the world disappears. When the power supply to the senses is withdrawn, the outer reality vanishes. What remains is the source.

That's when I understood what the Yoga Vasishtha keeps saying. *Consciousness is the only real thing*. That is also why I have distilled those

Consciousness Keys for you in every chapter. Everything else – this world, these sensations, these identities – they come and go. But the light within? It never leaves us. It is a real treasure.

Science may call itself the new religion. But it has focused far too long on studying the instruments of perception, and not enough on the power that runs through them. It's time to explore consciousness, for it is what enables perception itself.

To do this, we need to turn inwards and practice *pratyahara*, the gentle withdrawal of the senses, and to receive inner guidance from a spiritual guide who has walked this path. We can certainly try on our own, but with a guide, the journey is swifter and simpler. This is what Krishna gave to Arjuna, and what Vasishtha gave to Ram: a transmission of *pranahuti*, the living vibration of Reality that we know today as yogic transmission.

Reading the Yoga Vasishtha helped to create interest. But it was my guru's transmission that made me experience the soul. The stories came alive and the treasure revealed itself. So I say to you, if you're a seeker, try this experiment: Meditate with a Heartfulness trainer. Let transmission awaken the stillness in you. And then witness the magic and miracles for yourself.

Let this book be a beginning.

May it lead you to the Source.

May you find the real treasure within.

With love,
Daaji

Appendices

Appendix 1: Heartfulness Relaxation

Read through these guided suggestions and try them on yourself or read them aloud to help guide others.

- Sit comfortably and close your eyes very softly and very gently.
- Feel the healing energy of Mother Earth move up into your toes, feet and ankles. Then up to your knees, relaxing the lower legs.
- Begin with your toes. Wiggle them. Now feel them relax.
- Feel the healing energy move further up your legs. Relax your thighs.
- Now, deeply relax your hips, lower body and waist.
- Relax your back. From your tailbone to your shoulders, feel your entire back relaxing.

- Relax your chest and shoulders. Feel your shoulders simply melting away.
- Relax your upper arms. Relax each muscle in your forearms, your hands and right to your fingertips.
- Relax your neck muscles. Move your awareness up to your face. Relax your jaw, mouth, nose, eyes, earlobes, facial muscles, forehead, all the way to the top of your head.
- Feel your whole body completely relaxed. Scan your system from top to toe, and if there is any part of your body that is still tense, painful or unwell, feel it being immersed in the healing energy of Mother Earth for a little while longer.
- When you are ready, move your attention to your heart. Rest there for a little while. Feel immersed in the love and light in your heart.
- Remain still and become absorbed within.
- Remain absorbed for as long as you want, until you feel ready to come out.

Appendix 2: Heartfulness Meditation

Choose a place where you can meditate without being distracted, preferably at the same place and same time daily. The most ideal time of day is before sunrise. Turn off your phone and other devices. Sit with your back upright but not rigid.

- Sit comfortably. Gently close your eyes and relax.
- If needed, take a couple of minutes to relax your body by doing the Heartfulness relaxation.
- Turn your attention inwards and take a moment to observe yourself.
- Then, suppose that the source of divine light is already present within your heart and that it is attracting you from within.
- Gently relax into that feeling. If you find your awareness drifting to other thoughts, do not fight them but do not entertain them either. Let them be, while simply reminding yourself that you are meditating on the source of divine light in your heart.
- Allow yourself to become more and more absorbed within.
- Remain absorbed within this deep silence for as long as you want, until you feel ready to come out of meditation.

Appendix 3: Heartfulness Cleaning

Do cleaning practice at the end of your day's work, preferably not too close to bedtime. This process will rejuvenate you and purify your system of any accumulated heaviness. There are a few steps to the process, so in the beginning, it is best to practice them in the following sequence:

- Sit in a comfortable position with the intention to remove all the impressions accumulated during the day.
- Close your eyes and relax.
- Imagine all the complexities and impurities are leaving your entire system.
- Let them flow out from your back in the form of smoke, from the area between your tailbone and the top of your head.
- Remain alert during the entire process without brooding over the thoughts and feelings that arise. Try to remain witness to your thoughts.
- Gently accelerate this process with confidence and determination.
- If your attention drifts and other thoughts come to mind, gently bring your focus back to the cleaning.

- As the impressions are leaving from your back, you will start to feel lighter.
- Continue this process for up to twenty to twenty-five minutes.
- When you feel light within, you can start the second part of the process.
- Feel a current of purity coming from the source entering your system from the front. This current is flowing into your heart and throughout your system, saturating every particle.
- You have now returned to a more balanced state. Every particle of your body is emanating lightness, purity and simplicity.
- Finish with the conviction that the cleaning has been completed effectively.

Appendix 4: Heartfulness Prayer

This prayer is offered at bedtime as a way of connecting to the Source before sleep. This may take around ten to fifteen minutes. It is also offered before meditation in the morning.

At bedtime, sit comfortably, gently close your eyes and relax. Silently and slowly repeat the words of the prayer below. Meditate for ten to fifteen minutes over the true meaning, feeling the words resonate in your heart rather than trying to analyse them. Let the meaning surface from within. Try to get lost in it. Go beyond the words and let the feeling come to you.

> O Master!
> Thou art the real goal of human life.
> We are yet but slaves of wishes
> putting bar to our advancement.
> Thou art the only God and Power
> to bring us up to that stage.

Now silently repeat these words a second time and go even deeper into this feeling. Allow yourself to be absorbed in it beyond the words. Allow yourself to melt in this prayerfully meditative state as you go to sleep.

In the morning, reconnect yourself by silently offering this prayer once before you start the Heartfulness meditation.

Appendix 5: Guided Regulation of Speech

- Sit comfortably and relax.
- Go into your heart. You may meditate for a few minutes to connect with your higher Self and deepen your condition.
- Now stay connected with your higher Self as you speak.
- Observe the tone of your conversation and let it flow evenly.
- To do this, remove any rise and fall in the pitch, sharpness or roughness.
- Attune your speech to the balanced condition of your heart.
- See if you can feel a relationship establishing with the original current within you.
- With time, your speech will become soft, cultured and smooth like the harmonious flow of divine grace. When your speech is in tune with that, you will naturally touch the hearts of others.
- Practice consciously and regularly to make this a permanent habit. Prevention is always better than cure.

Appendix 6: Guided 'Ocean of Peace' Cleaning

- Sit comfortably and close your eyes.
- Imagine that you are in a gentle ocean of peace. The waves are soothing and blissful.
- Have the firm thought that you are immersed in this ocean of peace, and the waves are removing all your coverings.
- Do this for as long as you can, but no more than thirty minutes.

Appendix 7: Guided Inquiry

- What situations and conditions create fantasy or fear in you?
- What memories and imaginary situations create negative emotions or imagined emotions in you?
- What are the worst imagined emotions that you have had?
- Do you know why you feel these imagined emotions? (If you do not know the real cause, that is okay.)
- Write your discoveries in your journal.

Appendix 8: Left-Nostril Breathing

- Relax your body and mind.
- Close your right nostril with your right thumb.
- Smile while you breathe.
- Slowly inhale through your left nostril and exhale through the same, breathing deep into your abdomen.
- Repeat this nine more times.

Appendix 9: Guided Limb Cleaning

- Imagine the divine current is flowing from above you.
- Draw the current down to your heart.
- Now let this current move towards your left shoulder, then let it descend down your arm to your biceps, your elbow, your wrist, your hand and flow out through the fingertips of your left hand.
- While this flow is going on, think that heaviness, complexities, impurities and fears are going out of your system along with the flow.
- Continue this process for two to three minutes, then gently taper the flow.

- Now again let the divine current be drawn down from above your head to your heart, and let it continue down through your left lower torso, through your left thigh and knee, down to your left foot and out through the toes of your left foot.
- While this flow is going on, think that heaviness, complexities, impurities and fears are going out of your system along with the flow.
- Continue this process for two to three minutes and then gently taper the process.
- Bring your attention once again above your head and allow the current to flow down to your heart. From the heart, divert it to your right shoulder and down your right arm all the way to your fingertips. It should be a very gentle process. Continue this process for two to three minutes and then gently taper the process.
- Then do the same thing on the right side from above your head to your heart, and then down through your torso and down your right leg to your right foot.
- When this energy is flowing out through the toes of your right foot, be sure to remove any heaviness from the right big toe.

- Repeat the whole process one more time if you feel that there is still fear or heaviness in your system.
- At the end, with confidence, affirm that you are completely cleaned of all fears and complexities, and that purity and simplicity are restored.

Appendix 10: Seeding Positive Thoughts

- Sit comfortably and close your eyes.
- Imagine the form of the person in front of you.
- Have the thought that they are your friend and well-wisher.
- Think that all negative thoughts the person has about you are going, and thoughts related to your welfare have been infused in them instead.
- Whenever you have the opportunity to go near the person, gently and subtly pay attention very indirectly to their face, without staring.
- When you breathe out, have the thought that particles of your love and affection are entering their heart.
- When you breathe in, have the thought that you are pulling all the negative thoughts they have

about you from their heart and throwing them aside.

- Initially this task may seem difficult and you may feel resistance, but if you are courageous, it will become easy as you practice it.

Appendix 11: Prayerful Suggestions

Suggestion 1

Everything surrounding us – the air particles, the people, the birds, the trees – is deeply absorbed in godly remembrance. All are in osmosis with the Source, and developing increased peacefulness and moderation.

Suggestion 2

Everyone is developing correct thinking, right understanding and an honest approach to life. They are attaining rightness in action and perfection in character.

Suggestion 3

Everyone is being filled with love and devotion and real faith is growing stronger in them. Truth and righteousness are getting established in the world. All kinds of distractions faced by our countries and our globe are going away. May this entire earth be engulfed with peace, love and divine grace.

Appendix 12: Creating Cheerful Acceptance

- Sit in a comfortable position.
- Gently close your eyes and bring your attention to your heart. Dive as deep as you can within your heart.
- Feel your heart's ability to accept everything, and let that acceptance spread through you. Notice the vacuum that is created when you are able to create acceptance.
- Invoke the presence of the divine, which will naturally flow into the vacuum.
- Go deeper into that state of acceptance.
- Allow the presence of the divine to expand within you.

- While deeply absorbed in the divine, ask for forgiveness for any mistakes you may have committed, even unknowingly. Resolve not to repeat them again.
- Stay in this state of repentance, with total self-acceptance, for a few minutes.
- Then connect yourself to your higher Self using the following prayer slowly and silently. Let the words resonate in the vacuum of your heart.

> O Master!
> Thou art the real goal of human life.
> We are yet but slaves of wishes
> putting bar to our advancement.
> Thou art the only God and Power
> to bring us up to that stage.

- Try to understand the meaning of the words in this offering of prayer, contemplate upon their meaning and remain absorbed with this prayerful state, which will also help you to go to sleep more easily.

Appendix 13: Being In Constant Remembrance

Constant remembrance is a way of staying connected to the presence of the divine in the heart throughout the day. It is not a separate task but becomes a part of how you think and act.

- At the beginning of the day, close your eyes and bring your attention to your heart.
- Suppose that the source of light within your heart is guiding your thoughts and actions today.
- After this, continue with your daily work. Keep this awareness of the heart as you speak, decide and act.
- Before starting any activity, pause for a moment. Feel the presence in your heart and then proceed.
- During breaks, such as before meals or while walking, remember the connection or attention that you have in the heart.
- This is not a mantra or a practice. It is just an interest and a consistency in being conscious of the divinity in your heart.
- With regular effort, your mind becomes less distracted and your choices become more deliberate.

- You begin to respond with more care, honesty and discipline in everyday situations.
- Keep refining this condition daily through simple observation and effort.

Appendix 14: Universal Prayer

The universal prayer is a daily Heartfulness practice that is dedicated to the welfare of all. At 9.00 p.m. sharp, everyone who would like to do so, wherever they might be at the time, may meditate for fifteen minutes, thinking that all brothers and sisters are being filled with love and devotion and that real faith is growing stronger in them. It shall be of immense value to them, which their practical experience only shall reveal.

Appendix 15: Heartfulness Meditation Sessions

Individual meditation sessions with a certified Heartfulness trainer can be sought through the below means:

Heartfulness App

Meditate for fifteen minutes a day with an instructor to bring about transformation in life. Take advantage of the Guided Exercises available for free on the Heartfulness app.

Available in the App Store and Play Store at hfn.link/app.

Connect Directly with a Heartfulness Instructor

To experience the Heartfulness practices first-hand, please contact a trainer at one of our centres, known as HeartSpots, by visiting heartspots.heartfulness.org, or download our mobile app to request a trainer online.

Follow the three introductory masterclasses online at hfn.li/masterclass.